Black Trilogy Plus

Also by Dorothy Swygert

A.G. Gaston: Portrait of a Dream

Healing the Nation

The Oak Leaf

The March for Justice

I Am Somebody (Character Building)

Black Trilogy Plus

A collection of plays on different eras in African American life and history

Lest We Forget	1860s
Black Renaissance	1915-39
The Montgomery Bus Boycott	1955

—Plus—

Rendition of the Negro Mother	1940s
The Reunion	1960s

Dramatic Productions by

Dorothy R. Swygert

REKINDLE THE HEART, HAMPTON, VIRGINIA, 2009

Printed in the United States of America

Book design and typography:
Studio E Books, Santa Barbara, CA
Maria Jonson, Copy Editor

ISBN 978-0-9648737-3-5

Library of Congress Control Number: 2009910627

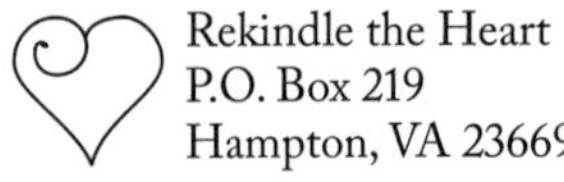
Rekindle the Heart
P.O. Box 219
Hampton, VA 23669

Contents

I. Lest We Forget 9
II. Black Renaissance 43
III. The Montgomery Bus Boycott 67
IV. The Negro Mother 87
V. The Reunion 97

Addendum

Don't Quit 143
Lord Why Did You Make Me Black? 144
God Answered 146

Resources for Young People 149

INTRODUCTION

Fortunately, for the reader, author Dorothy Swygert knows that all the world really is a stage, and that no drama being played out upon it is more engrossing than that of the African transplanted and enslaved, overcoming the "slings and arrows of outrageous fortune" to become the African American triumphant in the New World.

Black Trilogy is a collection of three plays whose *modus operandi* is in-your-face, with admirable restraint. The plays are subtly unsettling but, at the last, always temperate and satisfying. They are audience-centered and performer-focused. *In Black Family: It's Praying Time Lest We Forget From Whence We've Come*, the audience is compelled to uncomfortably hear out slave master Shannon's cruel rationalization of the eerie brutality with which he manages his slaves. The performer faces the challenge of engaging an audience that is immediately alienated and hostile toward his starring role. *In Black Renaissance: The New Negro*, 1915–1939, the smarting audience is transported to the interior life of Harlem USA, to the Christian choral stage, the daytime classroom, and to the nighttime hot spots; to the Cotton Club of the roaring 20s, the swinging cafes of the 30s, and to the jazz-filled ballrooms on the threshold of the 40s, where it encounters, among others, Lena Horne, Langston J. Hughes, James Weldon Johnson, Louis Armstrong and Margaret Walker. The performer faces the challenge of reintroducing us to the African American legends whose lives helped extricate an oppressed people from old exploitation south, to new expectations north. He must recite the poetry, play the music, dance the steps and sing the songs that are an integral part of the African American's freedom epic. In *The Montgomery Bus Boycott*, the audience confidently puts on the whole armor of faith, hope and activism to sit with Rosa Parks where they want to get on the segregated southern bus and to walk with Martin Luther King down to the dangerous corners of the Civil Rights Movement. The performer faces the challenge of sharing the words and verbalizing the faith of the overcomers who fought for their own special kind of homeland security. These plays are splendidly audience-centered and compellingly performer-focused.

Ms. Swygert's intent is clearly to preserve via *Black Trilogy* the pride African Americans brought to their personal and collective emancipation and the price they were willing to pay to achieve it. The men and women, the high school and college students, the professional companies who will perform her works will have the unique experience of reenacting the African American struggle for others and the pleasure of identifying with their heritage in the best literary tradition. Schools and church groups and libraries placing *Black Trilogy* on their shelves will honor afresh the unknown and the well known, the students and the statesmen and all the wonderful heroes and heroines who have played center stage and worked backstage to inspire a work as excellent as these plays.

Dorothy Swygert is a talent destined to place an important collection of articles and poetry and books about the African American presence in American society on the shelves of American history and on the shelves of African American heritage hearts. In private life, Dorothy is an activist clergyperson, a widow, the mother of two sons and an educator with credentials from Tuskegee University and New York University.

—Etta May Ladson, B.A., M.A., M.P.S.

Etta May Ladson is the author of *Strange Land Songs* and eight other titles. She is the publisher at Jewelgate Press and the Director of the African Christian Teachers Association in New York City.

1. *Lest We Forget*

BLACK FAMILY: It's Praying Time

Lest We Forget From Whence We've Come!

Introduction

Black Family: "It's Praying Time" is a dramatic story of the slave institution in America prior to and after slavery as portrayed through the eyes of the slave master, the overseer and the black preacher.

Full Version

Act I: *Before the Dawn of Freedom*
- Scene 1: Slave Master Shannon
- Scene 2: Sojourner Truth
- Scene 3: Harriet Tubman
- Scene 4: Slave Overseer
- Scene 5: The Picnic: Slave Hanging
- Scene 6: The Black Preacher
- Scene 7: The Camp Meeting in the Swampland
Song: Steal Away

Act II: *The Dawn of Freedom*
- Scene 1: Slave Master Unveiling the Emancipation Proclamation
Overseer Reads the Proclamation to Slaves
- Scene 2: Black Preacher's Jubilee
Song: Pray, God Can Make a Way

Short Version

Act I: *Slavery*
- Scene 1: Master Shannon's Plantation
(Slaves in background)
Shannon's Introduction of Sojourner Truth and Harriet Tubman
Shannon's Introduction of the Overseer
Black Preacher's Secret Message to Slaves, "Steal Away"

- Scene 2: Old Swamp Meeting
Slave Group Singing "Steal Away, We're Gonna Pray"
First Speaker: "Where's Rev. Jeremiah Ezekiel"?

Anonymous: Woman and child on auction block, 1800s.
Photographs and Prints Division, Schomburg Center for Research in Black Culture, the New York Public Library, Astor, Lenox and Tilden Foundations.

Cast of Characters

NARRATOR:	
WILL SHANNON:	Slave master
JEREMIAH EZEKIEL:	Black preacher
BRODY WILKERSON:	Overseer
SOJOURNER TRUTH:	Runaway slave
HARRIET TUBMAN:	Runaway slave
WATERBOY:	
TOP HAT MAN:	Slave hanging
SORIAH:	Slave
SISTER SOOKIE:	Slave
MARY HENSON:	Slave
LEROY HENSON:	Slave
DAVID JONES:	Slave
HENRY JOE:	Slave
BROTHER BOB:	Slave
JOHNNY MAE:	Slave
BETH:	White mistress
SARAH:	White mistress

THEME: From Slavery to Freedom

MOOD: Black slaves are praying and waiting for the day of jubilee.

PLOT: Black preacher, in disguise, is secretly working with slaves to help them gain freedom.

SCENE: Virginia Plantation, MASTER WILL SHANNON

TIME: The 1860s

—ACT I—

Before the Dawn of Freedom

Scene 1

SETTING: *A Virginia plantation in the 1860s.*
AT RISE: *MASTER WILL SHANNON dressed as a wealthy planter, robust and well spoken, explains life on his plantation.*

SHANNON

Yeah, Shannon Plantation is mine, all 5,000 acres right in the heart of Virginia.

Takes pipe from his mouth and laughs.

I have about 300 slaves working my plantation.

Smiles proudly

I'm not like some of those mean slave owners. I treat my slaves very well.

Boastful tone

Why, I see that they get some food, some clothes, and a roof over their heads.

Pause

Now for my slave men, I give them two pairs of pants, two shirts, a jacket, and a pair of shoes for the season.

The women…

Smiles

I give a piece of muslin cloth for a gown. They don't need shoes 'til they're old enough to really work in the field!

Naughty smile as he walks around slowly.

Now there's a special gift for the slave women. I reward them every time they give birth to a youngun'.

Smiles

Why I give them a bright red piece of cloth for a new dress.

Sits on a stool and crosses his leg.

Food, yeah, I want my slaves to be well fed. I've given them a healthy ration of cornmeal, molasses and fatback. Why, I even provide them with a one-room dirt floor cabin.

Stands

Now, about grouping them, you got to be smart to keep peace on your plantation. The lighter complexion are my domestic slaves and they work in my Big House. Of course, that's where I live. I have the finest mahogany furniture that you can find around. I import my fine linen and silver from England. My floors are covered with oriental carpet, with silk and satin drapes and paintings throughout the house. Now, the darker complexion are the field slaves. They work in the fields from sun-up to sundown.

Smiles

Or better still, you can say that they work from "kin to can't."

Laughs wryly

From the time that they can see to the time that they can't see. Well now, don't get me wrong, why, I do believe in giving my slaves a good time.

Pause

At Christmas time I give them a day off and a keg of liquor so they can drink, play their music and be happy.

Walks around, a reflection of authority.

I've told you a lot about plantation life, but I must be very frank with you. Why, we slave masters, do have a very serious problem with those ornery slaves who are always wanting to run away. Even the women slaves try to run away. Why, I remember one slave master who lost one of his female slaves. Her name is still remembered, Sojourner Truth. We heard tell that she ran away up North and joined one of those famous abolitionist societies, you know, that group that try to get rid of our happy way of life.

BLACKOUT

END OF SCENE

Sojourner Truth and Abraham Lincoln.
Library of Congress Prints and Photos.

Act I, Scene 2

SETTING: *An Abolitionist meeting.*
AT RISE: *SOJOURNER TRUTH in standing facing the audience at the meeting. She is attired in a long black dress with a white-cloth front; tall and slender with a strong, clear voice.*

SOJOURNER

Who am I?

Looks out on audience

At birth, I was named Isabella! One day, the Lord touched me and changed my whole life. God touched me and from that day on I considered myself a "Pilgrim of God."

Pause

What is my mission?

Smiles

My mission is to speak out against slavery and its cruel institution. And speak out, I surely will!

Pause

Now, just let me tell you about my early life. Why, I was born a slave around 1797. I tell you, I could never get used to that life! So one day, I just took it upon myself to take my own freedom.

Smiles

You wondering how I did that?

Rubs her head with right arm with left hand resting on her waist.

Why, I just ran away! And in 1843, I started speaking out against slavery. I traveled from place to place and from state to state as a "Pilgrim of God" with one primary goal—to help set people free—free from slavery!

Pause

Yes, I met some white abolitionists like Parker Pillsbury and Harriet Beecher Stowe. I was even received in the White House by Abraham Lincoln.

Pause

Speaking out against slavery, my children, was not an easy task. Many times I was beaten and stoned. Oftentimes, I found myself sleeping wherever I could, eating barely enough to keep my body and soul in tack. But, I never forgot my God-given task, that was to speak out against slavery from a countless number of platforms.

Walks around, touching her banner across her chest.

I always wore a satin banner across my chest that read: "Proclaim liberty throughout the land unto all the inhabitants thereof." *(Lev. 25:10)*

Both hands on her waist.

Now I would like to share one old story with you.

Pause

One day I was out in this terrible weather, rain and mud. And I tell you, I was on my way to make one of my freedom speeches. But the weather was awful. The mud was so deep until I was getting stuck in the mud. And as I traveled, low and behold, there came a white gentleman riding on a big fine white horse.

Pause

And as he passed, he never once noticed me.

Pause

In fact, he galloped on his big fine horse and threw mud all over me. And I had to try to clean myself up the best way I could. So I took my bandanna from my head and tried to clean the mud off myself.

Pause

Then all of a sudden, this prissy, dainty white woman was out walking along, too. And all of a sudden she got stuck in the mud. Quickly, she started screaming, "Help, help!" And in a moment that same white man who had galloped by on the white horse, rode swiftly back to the defense of the white woman. He looked at the woman and said, "Miss, why are you out here? Don't you know that this is no kind of weather for a lady like you to be out in!"

Pause

Now when I got to the meeting place and was on the platform, I looked out in the audience and there was this same man. So when it was time for me to speak I told my story.

Hands akimbo, eyeglasses revealing poignant eyes, with commanding posture

I looked out upon the audience and I began.

Pause

As I was on my way to this convention, I was having a very difficult time trying to get through the mud and bad weather. I found myself getting stuck in the mud. It was becoming difficult for me to raise my foot out of the mud.

Pause—looks out into the audience and points to a man.

Now see that man out there!

Right arm extended, pointing.

Why, he was riding on his big white horse. It was bad enough that I was getting stuck in the mud, but when he came along, he galloped on his horse and slung more mud on me.

Pause

But then later, there was this prissy, little white woman who was trying to make her way through the mud and all of a sudden she got stuck. And she began screaming and crying out frantically "Help, help!" And as quick as a flash…

Points to the man in audience.

That same white man galloped back to the aid of this white woman and said: "Miss, why are you out in this kind of weather? This ain't no kind of weather for a lady to travel in." And immediately, he swept her upon his big fine white horse.

Pause

Now to that man out there in the audience, I tell you that I done plowed in the fields, I done picked cotton—and I done given birth to five children—*NOW AIN'T I A WOMAN, TOO!*

BLACKOUT

Fade back to SHANNON's Plantation.
SHANNON is seated in a chair with a pipe in his mouth.

SHANNON

Now if you think that Sojourner Truth was a character then, just sit still and let me tell you about Harriet Tubman.

Pause

Why, this slave ran away to freedom land, and believe me when I tell you that she was so tough until she kept coming back to the slave land, stealing slaves and taking them back to the North. I tell you she was so darn good until they started calling her Moses!

BLACKOUT

END OF SCENE

Fade scene to HARRIET TUBMAN.

Harriet Tubman.
Library of Congress Prints and Photos.

Act I, Scene 3

SETTING:
AT RISE: *HARRIET TUBMAN is dressed in a long dark dress carrying a shotgun by her side.*

TUBMAN

Who am I?

Pause

Can't you see that I'm that woman who is wanted throughout the South. You know they have a reward out for me!

Pause

Why? I don't know why, but I 'speck everybody wants freedom. I just like to help people leave slave land and go to freedom land. Now I ask you, is that a crime? Is anything wrong with trying to help someone to freedom...

Shrugs shoulders

Especially if they ain't done no wrong?

Pause

So now, you know who I am, the one who conducts the underground railroad and I run a safe train. Once you get your ticket, you don't get off until you get to freedom land. Yes, I am as mean and tough as the stories you've heard about me! I'm a shotgun-holding woman and I don't take nonsense from my passengers.

TUBMAN, facial expression of confidence and courage, leaning on her shotgun.

I'll tell you a true story about my underground railroad. You see, in order to ride my railroad, you had to be of good courage because I don't play.

Pause

On one of my trips going north to freedom, I had one slave, who got halfway, lost his nerve! Just got plain scared and he wanted to turn back.

TUBMAN looks down at her shotgun and continues speaking.

I looked this man dead in the eyes and I said,

Lifts up gun

If you turn around to go back south, I'll blow your head off!

Puts gun back at her side.

Ever since then, I never had no scared passenger riding on my train. The news got around that I run a smooth train to the North and I don't carry no jokers!

Looks at audience.

You can't blame me.

Wicked smile

If I'd let him go back, he would have left a trail that would have led to all of us, and that would not only be the end of the underground railroad, but the end of all of us!

Pause

Let me tell you about one other trip down South to my old ex-slave master. I knew they had a big reward out on me, but I didn't have time to let that frighten me. I had to pick up passengers for the underground railroad.

Laughs wryly

When I got to my old slave land, guess who I saw? Yeah, my old slave master! I had to think quick, I mean real quick.

Pause

I dressed down like a slave woman, old and sickly. I had a big basket on my left arm and when it was time to pass him, I had a couple of my chickens that I let fly out of the basket and I started to hobble and scramble, trying to catch the chickens.

TUBMAN winks her eye as she continues to tell the story.

Guess what old massa said? "Get 'em, granny, don't let 'em get away!" So, now you know why I was nicknamed Moses. You see, I run a smooth railroad underground, and I never lost a passenger!

TUBMAN puts right forefinger to her lips, "Shh!" and hobbles off stage.

BLACKOUT

Fade scene back to SHANNON's Plantation.

SHANNON

Smiles

Yes, that's Harriet Tubman. She's a smart, wicked chick who would snatch your slave before you could bat an eye, even in the broad open daylight.

Crosses his leg in a relaxed mood.

So running a plantation requires a lot of skill and a lot of know-how.

Points finger to his head.

Not bragging, but I've been running a strong plantation for years. And I tell you that I keep order on my plantation.

Laughs in a cynical manner.

And you know how I do that? I hire me a good, mean overseer.

SHANNON stops speaking abruptly. Overseer approaches.

Wait, he's coming out now!

Pause

Meet Brody Wilkerson!

BLACKOUT

END OF SCENE

Act I, Scene 4

SETTING: *At the SHANNON Plantation*

AT RISE: *BRODY WILKERSON, tall, lean, overly secure in personality. Walks through rows where slaves are working in the fields. Slaves are plowing, picking cotton and hoeing. Background music during his speaking.*

WILKERSON

Recites poem

POEM: "Overseer"

I'm the overseer on SHANNON plantation.
I carry out responsibilities beyond any imagination.

Slaves on this plantation have to be trained.
Believe me when I tell you, I keep a tight rein.

They have to be up at sunrise,
And never be out when the shadow dies.

There are two kinds of slaves—domestic and field,
And none of my power to them will I yield!

For I'm the overseer, powerful and strong.
I never fail to lash them when they do wrong.

If they leave the plantation they must have a pass
Or else they'll get a beating and a week's food fast,

People come from miles around to see slaves hanging on poles.
Other slaves will know what to expect if they don't play their roles.

The whip is needed to condition them all
So they'll answer the master's every beckon and call,

Fields to cultivate, cotton to pick,
Every slave will work whether well or sick.

The women are rewarded for having babes.
A human machinery to produce more slaves.

Two pairs of pants, a jacket and shoes they may get.
When they wear them out they need not fret.

Now I may sound tough and I may sound mean
But I run a plantation that is tops and supreme!

Looks around with a mean facial expression.

Where is that water boy?

Dressed in a sackcloth gown, WATER BOY rushes on stage barefoot with a pail of water.

WILKERSON looks at the WATER BOY with an authoritative expression.

Boy…

Finger pointed in WATER BOY's face.

Don't ever let me have to call you again! You keep up with me!

WATER BOY stands in humble position with head bowed.

Did you hear me?

WATER BOY

Yassa'.

WILKERSON

Turns to audience

You see, you have to train them, otherwise they'll grow up to be ornery, and the next thing you know, they'll be running away from your plantation.

Smiles

Why, I've only had to beat three of them to death.

Stands tall, chest elevated outward.

It may sound a little cruel, but you got to keep fear in them.

Smiles

And that's the best way that I know how to keep fear in them. Why, if you don't, they'll not only run away from your plantation, but will lead a rebellion against you, too!

Nervous expression

I remember that Nat Turner back in 1831. And I tell you, most of the other white folks remember him, too. It was a reign of terror. This slave thought he had received a vision from God to deliver the slaves from bondage to freedom and he organized a rebellion. I tell you that they went mad. They caught us white folks off guard and that Nat Turner group was killing every white person in sight. Finally, the slave masters and overseers got organized and didn't they catch that Nat Turner!

Smiles

Now this is what we do when we have an ornery slave like Nat Turner.

Looks out on audience and grins.

We pass the word throughout the countryside that we're gonna have a slave-hanging.

Pause

I tell you, the people come from miles and miles around with picnic baskets to watch this hanging.

BLACKOUT

END OF SCENE

Act I, Scene 5

SETTING: *Picnic hanging.*

AT RISE: *People are dressed in antebellum attire, long dresses and hats, carrying baskets. SARAH is carrying a picnic basket on her left arm, using right hand to fan.*

SARAH

You know Hennerson's slave got ornery enough to run away and knocked out his overseer before he escaped.

BETH

Walking side-by-side with SARAH

It's just getting to be so dangerous to keep slaves on your plantation.

Sarah

Now Beth, that is not all true. You just have to know how to treat slaves.

Beth

Matt Hudson has been having a lot of problems with his slaves, too.

Sarah

What kind of problems?

Beth

Would you believe that half of his slaves have already run away!

Sarah

Beth, that is what this hanging is about. We hang runaways and rebellious slaves in the Town Square. This will let other slaves know what will happen to them if they try to run away.

Crowd increases. Top Hat Man stands on an elevated platform rigged for hanging.

Top Hat Man

Ladies and gentlemen of Harpers Ferry County, Virginia, we're gathered here to make our home, our property, and our lives safe. And to fulfill this order we are here to witness the picnic hanging of Master Jergenson's slaves who attempted to escape from his plantation.

Pause

I'm going to ask Overseer Wilkerson to come down and talk to you a little about why we need to have slave hangings as a public event.

Crowd clap hands and cheer loudly with smiles, laughter, and grins.

Wilkerson makes his way to the front of the crowd.

Wilkerson

Recites poem

Poem: Slave Hanging

Now let me tell you what we do for the runaway slave.
We gather the people around and dig his grave.

Why we have to be strong and teach them not to forget
That when they disobey us, they'll pay a grave debt.

Now we had some slaves who led a rebellion.
The word went out to stop that hellion.

Before very long, we had caught the ornery blacks,
And pretty soon, we had them hanging on slats.

The people from miles and miles around came to see
What would happen to a slave who wants to be free.

They brought picnic baskets to celebrate the fun.
It'll be a long time before another slave decide to run.

The rope was tightened around each neck,
And the crowd cheered for the master's sake.

Now that's not being mean, it's just a lesson being taught
And if you fail to do it you, you just might get caught

By a rebellious slave who has a road to pave,
To teach other slaves how to misbehave.

BLACKOUT

END OF SCENE

Act I, Scene 6

SETTING: *At the SHANNON Plantation. Slaves working in the field.*

AT RISE: *REV. JEREMIAH EZEKIEL is dressed in black pants, white shirt, black hat and carrying a black Bible in his hand. While the preacher is talking, the slaves are in the background working. As they work, they secretly pass the word to steal away to the swamp meeting. Each slave steals away with singing in the background.*

REV. EZEKIEL

Recites poem

Who am I? I'm Jeremiah Ezekiel, the black preacher.
I ride from miles and miles, and you see, I'm the black preacher.
Oftentimes my job calls for me to even be a great teacher.

From plantation to plantation I ride
With the great Gospel news at my side.

The slave institution is a hard one, you see,
Built on a foundation that won't let blacks live free.

They work from sun up to sun down
And their slave masters describe them as simple little clowns.

But I carry the Gospel news to my brothers in bondage
And they've learned to trust in Him and give spiritual homage.

I tell you, one day the Lord is going to answer their cry.
The shackles of slavery will be broken by and by.

So I teach them to have faith, trust and to believe
For the burdens of slavery the Lord will soon relieve.

So I'm going to a great camp meeting in the deep dark swampland,
where we will sing, shout and pray with uplifted hands!

BLACKOUT

END OF SCENE

Act I, Scene 7

SETTING: *Camp meeting in the Swampland.*
AT RISE: *SLAVES enter swampland, peeping and looking around then begin to sing.*

SLAVES

Singing "Steal Away, We're Gonna Pray"

Steal Away, steal away, steal away, we're gonna pray,
Steal away, steal away, steal away, we're gonna pray,

A great camp meeting, a great camp meeting, a great camp meeting in the swampland,
A great camp meeting, a great camp meeting, a great camp meeting in the swampland,
We have no shoes, we have no shoes, but we've got the good Gospel News
We have no shocs, we have no shoes, but we've got the good Gospel News.

Steal away, steal away, steal away today and pray.
Steal away, steal away, steal away to Jesus!

SORIAH looks around, put hands on her face with an expression of stress and fear.

SORIAH

I mean child, I sho' had a hard time tryin' to get here tonight!

SLAVES

Yeah, yeah, but praise the Lord we made it.

SORIAH

Looks around, put hands on her face with an expression of stress and fear.

Where's Rev. Jeremiah Ezekiel? He said he was comin'. He's not here and I done slipped off that plantation and he ain't even much here! My shoes done wore out and my toes are frost bitten and things just ain't gettin' no better on that plantation. There's so much bad news. Why, just yesterday, Sister Eliza got sold down the river.

SLAVES pat her on her back to console her.

Janella

Sister Soriah, you just calm yourself right down. Rev. Ezekiel is gonna come.

Soriah

An expression of calm.

Alright then, I'll be patient. I'll wait on Rev. Ezekiel.

Janella

Looks around at the group.

Now let's just sing a little song 'til he comes.

Slaves

That's right, we'll just sing a few songs 'til he comes.

Brother Bob

Let's sing our old faith hymn "Gimme That Old Time Religion!"

Slaves

Sing "Give Me That Old Time Religion," as they clap hands.

Gimme that old time religion, gimme that old time religion *(Chorus)*
Gimme that old time religion, it's good enough for me. *(Chorus)*
It was good for my dear mother, it was good for my dear mother,
It was good for my dear mother, it's good enough for me.

It was good for my old father, it was good for my old father,
It was good for my old father, it's good enough for me.

It was good for Paul and Silas, it was good for Paul and Silas,
It was good for Paul and Silas, it's good enough for me.

It was good for the Hebrew children, it was good for the Hebrew children, it was good for the Hebrew children, it's good enough for me.

Brother Bob

These times are so hard, but we must keep the faith and we know God is with us. We'll sing "Nobody Knows the Trouble I See."

Slaves

Sings

Nobody knows the trouble I see, nobody knows but Jesus,
Nobody knows the trouble I see, Glory Hallelujah. *(Chorus)*

Sometimes I'm up, sometimes I'm down,
Oh yes, Lord. *(SLAVES)*
Sometimes, I'm almost to the ground,
Oh yes, Lord. *(SLAVES)*

Nobody knows the trouble I see, nobody knows, but Jesus,
Nobody knows the trouble I see, Glory Hallelujah. *(CHORUS)*

HENRY JOE

We pray that the preacher will be comin' soon. Maybe, he havin' a hard time tryin' to get here. So let's sing our special song, "Steal Away."

SLAVES

SLAVES fold their hands and walk around slowly in a circle and begin singing.

Steal Away
Steal away, steal away, steal away to Jesus!
Steal away, steal away home, I ain't got long to stay here.

My Lord, he calls me, he calls me by the thunder;
The trumpet sounds within my soul; I ain't got long to stay here.
Green trees are bending, poor sinners stand a trembling;
My Lord, He called me, He calls me by the lightning;

JANELLA

Looks around and smiles

There's Rev. Ezekiel!

SLAVES

God bless you, Rev. Ezekiel, we knew you would come! We been patiently waiting for you. We so glad you made it.

Members of the group speak at different times until all have spoken.

SORIAH

Rev. Ezekiel, slavery ain't gettin' no better. Cassie done got his face branded by his master just like you brand animals. And Henrietta, she got one hundred lashes on her back because she was caught tryin' to slip off the plantation. She couldn't make it tonight. I mean the blood was just streamin' down! Rev. Ezekiel, when is the Lord gonna answer our cry?

Rev. Ezekiel opens his mouth to speak, but before he can, the other slaves speak.

Mary Henson

And, Sister Sadie. Why Sister Sadie was tryin' to come and she tripped and fell in the creek.

Slaves

Solemn expression

Got drowned?

Mary Henson bows head in affirmative.

Slaves quickly covers their mouths in dismay and oohs with wild glazing eyes.

Johnnie Mae

In excited voice

Jasmine got his hand cut off because he was caught tryin' to steal a chicken to feed his family!

Slaves

Oh, Lord! Help us.

Leroy Henson

Hattie Lou children got sold down the river, all the way down to Georgia!

Slaves

Sympathetic expression

Oh no! Poor children!

Sister Sookie

We work from "kin to can't," from the time we can see to the time we can't see on a serving of corn mush, fatback and molasses.

Henry Gillen

Sam was caught off the plantation after dark without a pass and he got his leg cut off.

Pause

All the way up to here.

Demonstrates

DAVID

Rev. Ezekiel, we takin' a grave chance to come out here in this deep dark swampland to have a camp meetin'. And now we here and we want you to call on the Lord's name in the most mightiest way. Because we slaves are gettin' very tired. Some have already given up, but we still got hope, we still believe that the Lord will one day hear our cry.

REV. EZEKIEL

Pats DAVID on the back

God bless you.

Looks at the SLAVES and begins his text.

My faith believers in Christ, greetin's, greetin's to all a ya freedom seekin' people. I tell you that one day the Lord will make a way. He gonna take the whip out of that overseer's hand and help him to understand the Christian band.

Pause

I'm sorry to hear about Sister Sadie who tripped and fell in the creek! My heart aches to hear how old Jasmine got his hand chopped off because he was tryin' to take a chicken from the master's chicken yard to feed his family. It's troublesome to my soul to hear that Cassie got his face branded like an animal and my heart goes out to Hattie Lou whose children got sold down the river to Georgia, and I am sorry that Henrietta got a hundred lashes on her back for tryin' to run away.

Pause

But, my dear Christians, have faith. I tell ya that the Lord will make a way.

GROUP

Yes, yes, He will, He show 'nough will!

REV. EZEKIEL

And I want to tell ya that the meaner that slave master becomes, the greater ya faith should be in the Lord.

Looks at the bible in his hand.

The Good Book here tells us how the Lord has helped people.

SLAVES

Yeah, Rev. Ezekiel, just tell us, tell us about the goodness of the Lord.

REV. EZEKIEL

Well, my Christian children, I tell ya that the Lord was with Daniel in the lion's den and the power of the Lord was so great until he changed the lion into a gentle lamb.

Slaves

Amen, amen! Tell us more!

Rev. Ezekiel

I tell ya that the Hebrew boys were thrown into the fiery furnace and not one strain of their hair burned.

Slaves

Amen, Rev., Amen! Tell us a lil bit more!

Rev. Ezekiel

Well, I'll tell ya, my brothers and sisters in bondage, about the greatest revelation of freedom. Now ya know that the Children of Israel were held in bondage by the Egyptian Pharaoh, and they cried out unto the Lord, and the Lord, by and by, heard their cry.

Slaves

Amen, amen!

Rev. Ezekiel

I tell ya that the Lord's power is so great until He swept a path through the Red Sea, and the Children of Israel walked right through the sea on the path to freedom.

Slaves clap their hands in high spirits.

And my dear Christians, I wants to tell ya right here in this dark swampland, that the Lord is goin' to deliver ya from slavery in America. He's gonna remove ya from this plantation of slavery and uplift ya to the freedom of salvation!

Slaves

Praise the Lord! Praise the Lord!

Rev. Ezekiel

So just be patient, just keep on bearin' your burdens, for after while, by and by, when the mornin' come, ya gonna hear the freedom bell ring.

Slaves

Amen, Reverend, we gonna keep on waitin', gonna keep on hopin', we gonna keep on prayin' 'til He comes.

They shake Rev. Ezekiel*'s hand and pat him on the back as they crowd around him. They march out singing "Soon-a Will Be Done."*

Slaves

Sings

Soon-a will be done with the troubles of the world,
The troubles of the world, the troubles of the world,
Soon-a will be done with the troubles of the world,
Goin' home to live with God.

END OF ACT I

—ACT II—

The Dawn of Freedom

Scene 1

SETTING: *SHANNON's Plantation. Unveiling the Emancipation*

AT RISE: *WILL SHANNON, slave master, comes downstage to make the sad announcement. He sits on a stool with a cadaverous expression.*

SHANNON

Freedom. That's what the slaves wanted, and now their wish has come true!

SHANNON gets up and speaks slowly, but with an impact to be left on the audience.

Recites poem

POEM: Fading Glory

Now that President Lincoln done freed the slaves
And paved the way for slave masters' graves,

We have to call the slaves out and read them their rights.
If we disobey we're be involved in another fight.

Two hundred years, a fine way of life
Brought to an end by a sharp blade knife.

A hard war to fight, our wealth has grown thin,
A glorious way of life is gone with the wind!

SHANNON stands, puts hands in his pockets, then calls BRODY WILKERSON.

Brody! Brody! Come on out here. You know we have to obey the Union!

WILKERSON comes out, walking slowly with countenance of anger, carrying cap in his hand.

WILKERSON

Mr. Shannon, you called me?

SHANNON

Nods his head

The days of glory seem to have just faded in the wind.

WILKERSON

Throwing cap from one hand to the other.

Mr. Shannon, I just can't see why them slaves need to be free.

Pause

You know those slaves need someone to oversee their lives.

SHANNON

Brody, we got to obey that Emancipation Proclamation.

Pats BRODY on his back.

So you just round up the slaves and bring them on out here so I can read them their rights.

WILKERSON

Angry expression

The war is over and the curtain comes down
And now, I'm the only one who looks like a clown!

WILKERSON takes his hat and throws it down and exits the stage to get the SLAVES.

SLAVES enter stage in pairs, stand humbly with heads bowed.

SHANNON looks at the SLAVES with mixed feelings.

SHANNON

You know I've always done right about all of you. Y'all know I always saw to it that you had plenty of ration, clothes, and a roof over your head, and I always treated you kindly.

SLAVES' heads bow in affirmative with half- smile, eager to hear the words that they've already overheard.

Well...

Pause

You, you know that President Lincoln has passed his Emancipation Proclamation.

Pause

That's a mighty fancy word! Well, I'm to read this to all my slaves.

Pause

So, if you'd just listen carefully, I will read it to you.

Unrolls the scroll and begins reading.

"The Emancipation Proclamation
"By the President of the United States of America

"I, Abraham Lincoln, President of the United States of America, and Commander-in-Chief of the Army and Navy thereof, do hereby proclaim and declare that hereafter, as heretofore, the war will be prosecuted for the object of practically restoring the constitutional relation between the United States, and each of the states, and the people thereof, in which states that relation is, or may be suspended, or disturbed.

"That it is my purpose upon the next meeting of Congress to again recommend the adoption of a practical measure tendering pecuniary aid to the free acceptance or rejection of all slave states, so called, the people whereof may not then be in rebellion against the United States, and which states may then have voluntarily adopted, or thereafter may voluntarily adopt, immediate or gradual abolishment of slavery within their respective limits; and that the effort to colonize persons of African descent [with their consent of the Governments existing there] will be continued.

"That on the first day of January in the year of our Lord, one thousand eight hundred and sixty-three, all persons held as slaves within any state, or designated part of a state, the people whereof shall be in rebellion against the United States shall be then, thenceforward, and forever free; and the executive government of the United States [including the military and naval authority thereof] will recognize [and maintain the freedom of] such persons, and will do no act or acts to repress such persons, or any of them, in any efforts they may make for their actual freedom."

SLAVES are eager to shout jubilee, but reserve their joy of freedom, secretly touch each other and give half-smiles.

Now all those fancy words simply mean is that you are free.
Pause
You're welcomed to stay on with me and any of you who wish to stay on with me, I will do right 'bout you. I'll pay you a fair share.
Pause
I tell you it's a very hard life for everybody, now that the war is 'bout over.
Pause

Railroads are destroyed. Plantations have been run over and burned. There's barely work for anyone.

Pause

So, if you want to stay on, just come and let me know. I'll be in my study.

SHANNON leaves the stage.

BLACKOUT

END OF SCENE

Act II, Scene 2

SETTING: *On stage.*
AT RISE: *REV. EZEKIEL appears downstage with a big smile.*

REV. EZEKIEL

Recites poem

POEM: The Preacher's Promise Fulfilled

Now, I told ya the Lord would answer their cry.
The freedom from bondage came down from on high.

The great God Almighty heard our plea
And now, we thankin' him on bended knee.

The master's plantation lay desolate on the land.
This what happen when ya join the Christian band.

The mean overseer done lost his job
And now all he can do is to sit and sob.

When ya trust in the Lord and obey His command,
He will surely guide ya to the Promised Land!

SLAVES rush out to greet REV. EZEKIEL from upstage.

SLAVES
The Lord heard our cry, Rev. Ezekiel. Praise the Lord!

REV. EZEKIEL
My children, ah told ya that the Lord would answer our cry.

SLAVES
Amen, amen. Praise the Lord!

REV. EZEKIEL
Now just let us join in and sing a song to praise the Lord.

SLAVES
Clap hands and raise voices of jubilee
Amen, amen, Rev. Ezekiel. We gonna sing a song right now!

Sings

Pray. God Can Make a Way

He heard our cry, He answered our plea
And now we thank Him on bended knee.

He can move a mountain. He can hew down a tree.
God can do anything. He set me free!

Praise the Lord and give Him thanks.
We done come across Jordan Banks.

He can open a sea. He can light a trail.
God can do anything, but He can't fail.

Chorus: Pray, pray, pray to the Lord, He'll make a way.
Pray, pray, pray to the Lord, He'll make a way.

REV. EZEKIEL

Add prayer in your daily life. Pray before you retire to sleep. Pray when you arise in the morning. Gather the family members around the table and bless the food. Pray before going to work, to school, to business or anywhere.

BLACKOUT

THE END

II. *Black Renaissance*

Introduction

SETTING: *African Open Air Pavilion. Drums. Man in African attire rolls out the runner slowly to the end of stage. The KING's throne is majestic.*

AFRICAN ANNOUNCER

Loud, heavy voice

Oh, Great King!

GUARD with outstretched hand points in the direction of the KING's throne.

KING enters with his entourage and guards. Drums play until the KING has been seated.

KING

Clasping his hands

Decorate my court!

Fashion Scene: African models take positions. Models appear one at a time to the beat of the drums and take a specified position in the KING's court.

KING

Clasping his hand with authority

Bring out the dancers!

Dancers dressed in African attire dance to the beat of drums.

AFRICAN ANNOUNCER

Oh great king, we have a long, lost brother from America who would like to study history. His name is Alain Locke.

KING

A long, lost brother?

Pause

Show him in!

ALAIN LOCKE enters court slowly and bows to the KING.

KING stretches out his hand to indicate a sitting place to the right side of his court.

ALAIN LOCKE bows and sits to the KING's right.

KING

Be our honored guest!

ALAIN LOCKE

Bow to king

I am most honored.

Female servants offer platters of fruits to courtiers.

KING

A hand clap

Send forth my historian with a scroll of our glorious history!

ANNOUNCER leaves stage to get HISTORIAN.
SCRIBE enters. Stands attentively and waits for KING to speak.

KING

Read the history of this great land to our brother!

HISTORIAN

Yes, your majesty.

Unfolds scroll and beings to read.

There were three great West African kingdoms: Ghana, Mali and Songhay. Ghana was a country so rich in gold until the King's animals wore collars of gold. The ruler of Ghana was Tenkamenin. Mansa Musa was the ruler of Mali. The great kingdom of Songhay was Sunni Ali. People from Europe and all parts of the worlds traveled to trade in the great land of Africa.

Pause

Africa was not just rich in minerals and wealth but was the storehouse of knowledge. While Europe was still undeveloped, scientists in Africa were performing such delicate operations as removing cataracts from the eyes. Our people set the weights, the measures and the time. They were astute mathematicians and scientists. The embalming art is still the secret of this flourishing continent. The pyramids reach up to kiss the clouds, and the astrologers read the signs of the times. Poets like Alexander Pushkin query the soul for wisdom.

The curtains close while the HISTORIAN is still reading African history.

BLACKOUT

Cast of Characters

NARRATOR: THE OLD NEGRO

PAUL ROBESON

THE FISK JUBILEE SINGERS

FEMALE: "The Creation"

CLAUDE MCKAY: "If We Must Die"

LOUIS ARMSTRONG

"SHUFFLE ALONG CAST"

"OTHELLO" SCENE: Robeson

DEAN DIXON

THE MILL BROTHERS

THE EMPEROR JONES' CAST

BILL "BOJANGLES" ROBINSON

LENA HORNE (Cotton Club)

GEORGIA JOHNSON: "The Heart of a Woman"

MARGARET WALKER

WILLIAM GRANT STILL

WILLIAM DAWSON

THEME: The New Negro

SCENE: Harlem, New York

TIME: 1915-1939

The old Negro was more or less a formula instead of a human being. In slavery he was considered property with which the slave master could do whatever he wished: beat it, cripple it, sell it or kill it. The old Negro was depicted more like a working horse, a beast of burden. Cartoonists during this period of history portrayed the Negro as a strong, muscular, black man decapitated. The headless Negro was only fit to work and not to be educated. Therefore, slave masters made every effort to prohibit slaves from receiving an education. The old Negro was something to be kept in a designated place, the lowest rank in society. In slavery, there were the overseers and patty rollers. After the Civil War, the Ku Klux Klan was organized with the specific purpose of keeping blacks in their place, that is, an inferior status in American society.

Black Renaissance

SETTING: *Harlem, New York*
AT RISE: *A YOUNG MALE dressed in African attire walks out and sits at a plain table in a plain kitchen. The table is covered with a red and white checked table cloth. After a second he walks forward and recites "I, Too, Sing America."*

YOUNG MALE

Recites poem

POEM: "I, Too, Sing America" by Langston Hughes

I am the darker brother, *Endurance, A dream deferred.*
They send me to eat in the kitchen
When company comes,
But I laugh,
And eat well,
And grow strong.

Tomorrow, *Hope, Dreams*
I'll be at the table
When company comes.
Nobody'll dare
Say to me,
"Eat in the kitchen,"
Then.

Besides, *Perseverance Pride in accomplishment*
They'll see how beautiful I am
And be ashamed—

I, too, am America.

BLACKOUT

Narrator

The 1920's introduced a new mood in America among blacks. Dr. Alain Locke, a black man, wrote about this historical period in America. He was born in Philadelphia, Pennsylvania and received his Ph.D. from Harvard University in 1918. Thirsty for knowledge, Dr. Locke studied at Oxford University in England and at the University of Berlin in Germany. He taught philosophy at Howard University until 1953.

Pause

Dr. Alain Locke initiated the "Black Renaissance." In 1925, he published *The New Negro*, a collection of poems, stories and essays. He observed the new pride that was developing in black people. There were no longer the "Black Sambo," Uncle Tom, mammy and auntie images as illustrated by the old Negro. That image depicted the Negro as a strong black man without a head. Now blacks were perceived in a different light, as thinking human beings, capable of making contributions to America and the world. The stereotypes were quickly being replaced with a new sense of dignity in Harlem, New York.

Pause

Dr. Locke traveled extensively in many countries. Once he returned from Europe with a priceless collection of ancient African art to be put on exhibit in America. Because of his great interest and profound research in black culture, Dr. Alain Locke is renowned as "The Father of the Black Renaissance."

Pause

Dr. Locke said that for many years blacks were ashamed of their religious music, and for generations the Negro Spirituals were disguised as Wesleyan hymn harmony. However, during the Black Renaissance, they were reintroduced with new meaning and cultural pride. The songs that once inspired their ancestors during the period of bondage were now packaged as heirlooms to be transmitted from generation to generation, testimony to the Lord for deliverance from slavery to freedom.

Pause

Paul Robeson was a brilliant scholar and singer. Ladies and gentlemen, the music of Paul Robeson!

Male Singer sings "Old Man River" and other songs in a deep voice, dressed in majestic African attire.

Narrator

Another great representative of the Black Renaissance was James Weldon Johnson. Born in Jacksonville, Florida, he was educated at Atlanta University. After completing his studies in law, he passed the exam and was admitted to the bar in Florida. Later he decided to go to New York. New York was a fast-growing cultural center, and for blacks it was the home of the Harlem Renaissance. He and his brother, Rosamond Johnson, wrote musical plays and songs for the Broadway stage and attended graduate school at Columbia University.

Pause

James Weldon Johnson edited two anthologies, one of black poetry and another of spirituals. He published two books of poetry. His most famous literary work is *God's Trombone*, a collection of seven sermons with an opening prayer. "The Creation," from *God's Trombone*, is one of his most accomplished literary pieces. Now we will open the curtains to the recitation and dramatization of "The Creation."

ORATOR is downstage, five creative dancers are upstage. Dancers are dressed in long flowing rainbow-colored chiffon with white leg dress.

ORATOR recites the complete poem. The dancers dramatize in the background.

ORATOR

Recites poem

POEM: "The Creation" by James Weldon Johnson
(A Negro Sermon from *God's Trombone*)

And God stepped out on space,
And he looked around and said:
I'm lonely—
I'll make me a world.

And far as the eye of God could see
Darkness covered everything,
Blacker than a hundred midnights
Down in a cypress swamp.

Then God smiled,
And the light broke,
And the darkness rolled up on one side,
And the light stood shining on the other,
And God said: "That's good!"

Then God reached out and took the light in His hands
God rolled the light around in His hands
Until He made the sun;

And He set that sun a-blazing in the heavens.
And the light that was left from making the sun
God gathered it up in a shining ball
And flung it against the darkness.

Spangling the night with the moon and stars,
Then down between
The darkness and the light
He hurled the world;
And God said: That's good!

Then God himself stepped down—
And the sun was on His right hand,
And the moon was on His left;
The stars were clustered about His head,
And the earth was under His feet.
And God walked, and where He trod
His footsteps hollowed the valleys out
And bulged the mountains up.

Then He stopped and looked and saw
That the earth was hot and barren.
So God stepped over to the edge of the world
And He spat out the seven seas—
He batted His eyes, and the lightning flashed—
He clapped His hands, and the thunders rolled—
And the waters above the earth came down,
The cooling waters came down.

Then the green grass sprouted,
And the little red flowers blossomed,
The pine tree pointed his finger to the sky,
And the oak spread out his arms,
The lakes cuddled down in the hollows of the ground,
And the rivers ran down to the sea;
And God smiled again,
And the rainbow appeared,
And curled itself around His shoulder.

Then God raised His arm and He waved His hand
Over the sea and over the land,
And He said: Bring forth! Bring forth!
And quicker than God could drop His hand,

Fishes and fowls
And beasts and birds.

Swam the rivers and the seas,
Roamed the forests and the woods,
And split the air with their wings,
And God said: That's good!

Then God walked around,
And God looked around
On all that He had made.
He looked at His sun,

And He looked at His moon,
And He looked at His little stars;
He looked on His world
With all its living things,
And God said: I'm lonely still.

Then God sat down—
On the side of a hill where He could think;
By a deep, wide river He sat down;
With His head in His hands,
God thought and thought,
Till He thought: I'll make me a man!

Up from the bed of the river
God scooped the clay;
And by the bank of the river
He kneeled Him down;
And there the great God Almighty
Who lit the sun and fixed it in the sky,
Who flung the stars to the most far corner of the night,
Who rounded the earth in the middle of His hand;
This Great God,
Like a mammy bending over her baby,
Kneeled down in the dust
Toiling over a lump of clay
Till He shaped it in His own image;

Then into it He blew the breath of life,
And man became a living soul.
Amen. Amen.

Narrator

Fisk University is an educational institution that was constructed after the Civil War for black students. By 1871, the school was faced with financial problems. There was also the even greater threat, the closing of the university. However, the treasurer of Fisk, George White, took great interest in preserving this historic institution. He had a creative idea to increase funds. He organized a Fisk chorus to sing Negro spirituals, and on October 6, 1871, the Jubilee Singers began their tour of the United States. These singers performed under the direction of George White. He was not interested in the "minstrel singers" image where blacks had been presented as ragged singing clowns. They were refined and performed in a classical style which reflected their culture and heritage.

Pause

After touring America, the size of this chorus was decreased from twelve to eight to take a tour of Europe. The Jubilee Singers appeared before royal guests and were an overwhelming success. In 1878, they returned to America with a sum of one hundred and fifty thousand dollars to keep Fisk University open. They had done more than earned money to save the school. They had introduced the Negro Spirituals to the world.

Pause

We will be honored with a selection of Fisk Jubilee music.

The music may be performed by a chorus, a group or a choir.

Narrator

In 1922, the Black Renaissance was further enhanced by a book of poems, *Harlem Shadows*, by Claude McKay. After the Civil War, blacks were at the mercy of the Ku Klux Klan and other hate groups who were bitter about the abolition of slavery. Several of them were vicious in demonstrating their resentment of the Thirteenth Amendment to the Constitution. Their anger and bitterness frequently drove them to burn and destroy property belonging to blacks. Sadly, legal officials, like the president and policemen, turned their heads and refused to enforce the laws that protected the rights of the newly freed slaves. In response to these various incidents, Claude McKay wrote poetry to stimulate a more courageous people. His poem, "If We Must Die," is reflective of this historical period and appears in his book, *Harlem Shadows.*

Pause

Ladies and gentlemen, as you tune your heart to this poem, let your mind reflect on the experiences that inspired his writing "If We Must Die!"

A Young Man with a serious demeanor holding tools of defense enters.

Anonymous: 75th Jubilee Anniversary, Jackson State College, Jackson, Mississippi, Oct. 19–24, 1952.

Back row, left to right: Arna Bontemps, Melvin B. Towson, Jackson State College President, Jacob Radix, Owen Dodson, Robert Hayden.
Front Row, left to right: Sterling Brown, Zora Neale Hurston?, Margaret Walker, Langston Hughes.

Photographs and Prints Division, Schomburg Center for Research in Black Culture, the New York Public Library, Astor, Lenox and Tilden Foundations.

YOUNG MAN

Recites poem

POEM: "If We Must Die" by Claude McKay

If we must die—let it not be like hogs
Hunted and penned in an inglorious spot,
While round us bark the mad and hungry dogs,
Making their mock at our accursed lot.
If we must die—oh, let us nobly die,
So that our precious blood may not be shed
In vain; then even the monsters we defy
Shall be constrained to honor us though dead!
Oh, Kinsmen! We must meet the common foe;
Though far outnumbered, let us show us brave,
And for their thousand blows deal one deathblow!
What though before us lies the open grave?
Like men we'll face the murderous, cowardly pack,
Pressed to the wall, dying, but fighting back!

NARRATOR

An outstanding black female poetess, Georgia Johnson, received her degree from Atlanta University. She was the first woman after Frances Harper to gain recognition as a poet. Mrs. Johnson's poetry sings with emotion. Most of her works are love lyrics that tenderly touch the heart. Her three volumes of poetry include *The Heart of a Woman* in 1918, *Bronze* in 1922 and *An Autumn Love Cycle* in 1928.

Pause

A YOUNG WOMAN sits at her desk, in a pensive mood. There is a voice backstage or tape recorded while she holds her paper reading silently, or have the writer recite the poem.

YOUNG WOMAN

Recites poem

POEM: "The Heart of a Woman" by Georgia Johnson

The heart of a woman goes forth with the dawn,
As a lone bird, soft winging, so restlessly on,
Afar o'er life's turrets and vales does it roam
In the wake of those echoes the heart calls home.

Anonymous: [Silent Protest parade on Fifth Avenue, New York City, July 28, 1917, in response to the East St. Louis race riot. In front row are James Weldon Johnson [far right], W.E.B. DuBois [2nd from right], Rev. Hutchens Chew Bishop, rector of St. Philip's Episcopal Church [Harlem] and realtor John E. Nail.]

Photographs and Prints Division, Schomburg Center for Research in Black Culture, the New York Public Library, Astor, Lenox and Tilden Foundations.

The heart of a woman falls back with the night,
And enters some alien cage in its plight,
And tries to forget it has dreamed of the stars,
While it breaks, breaks, breaks on the sheltering bars.

NARRATOR

The Black Renaissance was characterized by blacks participating in theaters. Charles Gilpin played the leading role in Eugene O'Neill's *The Emperor Jones.*

Pause

Langston Hughes, born in Joplin, Missouri, began writing at an early age. He was named the class poet upon graduation from the eighth grade in Lincoln, Illinois. Hughes continued writing poetry. He had the opportunity of meeting Vachael Lindsay and other poets. He was greatly influenced by the writings of Walt Whitman and Carl Sandburg. As a poet, he studied history and culture and wrote about many of his life experiences. One of his most famous poems captures the struggles of black women trying to nurture boys to survive in a new generation.

Pause

Ladies and gentlemen, Langston Hughes' most famous poem, "Mother To Son."

FEMALE dressed as a struggling mother of the 1920s in a long cotton skirt, scarf neatly tied around her head and an apron around her waist. Her son is dressed in the same period, depicting difficult times. Mother's countenance is of courage, strength and hope. As curtain opens, mother stands, talking to her little son, giving him instructions in life-surviving skills.

FEMALE

recite poem

POEM: "Mother to Son" by Langston Hughes

Well, son, I'll tell you!
Life for me ain't been no crystal stair.
It's had tacks in it,
And splinters,
And boards torn up
And places with no carpet on the floor—
Bare.

Anonymous: Langston Hughes at Tuskegee Institute with Jessie Fauset (left) and Zora Neale Hurston, one year after his first book was published.
Photographs and Prints Division, Schomburg Center for Research in Black Culture, the New York Public Library, Astor, Lenox and Tilden Foundations.

But all the time
I'se been a'climbin' on,
And reachin' landin's,
And turnin' corners,
And sometimes goin' in the dark
Where there ain't been no light.

So boy, don't you turn back.
Don't you set down on the steps
'Cause you finds it kinder hard.

Don't you fall now—
For I'se still goin', honey,
I'se still climbin',
And life for me ain't been no crystal stair.

NARRATOR

The Black Renaissance was characterized by music in the jazz style introduced to Broadway by Fletcher Henderson and Louis Armstrong.

Pause

We honor the work of "Satchmo" by having two musicians play "West End Blues"" and "The St. Louis Blues."

Two male performers or a complete band play the music of Louis "Satchmo" Armstrong.

NARRATOR

The Black Renaissance was illustrious for black dancers who captured the attention of a large population. They created new dances like the Charleston, the Lindy Hop and the Cake Walk which became very popular and spread to many cities and states.

Pause

Ladies and gentlemen, that famous dance of the Roaring Twenties, The Charleston!

Five DANCERS enter in designer attire that reflects the dress during this period—the short chemise fringe dresses, pearls, elaborate headdress, period jewelry, stockings and dance shoes.

Director may use the same five females from The Creation, Models from the African Court Scene and the Charleston or prepare three different groups.

Dance number: The Charleston.

NARRATOR

Black talent was really blossoming. White society had its Freddy Astaire, but Harlem had its own dancer, Bill "Bojangles" Robinson.

Tap dancer dressed in a white suit with a black top hat, a black cane to complement his attire, white gloves and tap dance shoes.

If you do not have a male tap dancer, a female can do as well.

Tap dance as Bill "Bojangles" Robinson.

NARRATOR

The many forms of segregation and discrimination had locked blacks from white social circles. Black men used their barbershops as places for social gathering and communication. From haircutters' shops emerged a famous quartet known as The Mills Brothers.

Pause

We present to you a group who will perform some songs from The Mills Brothers.

Barbershop Scene: Four high chairs, barber tools, shaving cream and powder. Curtain opens with men placing shaving cream on customers. As they are engaged in small talk, they decide to get up and sing.

MILLS BROTHER

Hey, brother, let's do one of our numbers.

BROTHER

We don't mind. Which one?

MILLS BROTHER

You know our favorite one, "If I Didn't Care."

The group gets up with shaving cream on their face and sing.

NARRATOR

Black novels were also published during this period—Wallace Thurman's *The Blacker the Berry*, Claude McKay's *Banja* and Countee Cullen's sensational and stirring *The Black Christ*.

Pause

The Black Renaissance in Harlem was a glorious age, and its influence spread to many cities and states. By 1929, the Depression was creating hard times for people in America, thus affecting the pomp and splendor of this cultural awakening. However, some progress was made in the 1930s when President Franklin D. Roosevelt endeavored to revive the country from depression with the New Deal program. The Federal Writer's project evolved from this economic plan. Some black poets and writers like Margaret Walker, Richard Wright and Arna Bontemps were employed with this project. In 1931, Arna Bontemps published *God Sends Sunday*. Sterling Brown, another writer, served as an advisor to new writers and artists.

Pause

Margaret Walker, a native of Birmingham, Alabama, had the opportunity to meet several writers on this project. She, too, became affiliated with the Federal Writers Project. A prolific writer, Ms. Walker captured the mood, history and culture of blacks amid this cultural transformation.

Pause

We will be favored with a recitation and dramatization of this beloved poem, "For My People."

As poem is recited, a group dramatizes the various facets of the black experience with their dress to reflect the times: some ironing, washing, working in the field, and chopping and when the Speaker *says in the last paragraph, "Let a new earth arise, a new generation be born..." a male and female enter with graduation attire to represent the new generation.*

Speaker

Recites poem

Poem: "For My People" by Margaret Walker

For my people everywhere singing their slave songs repeatedly; their dirges and their ditties and their blues and jubilees, praying their prayers nightly to an unknown god, bending their knees humbly to an unseen power;

For my people lending their strength to the years, to the gone years and the maybe years, washing, ironing, cooking, scrubbing, sewing, mending, hoeing, plowing, digging, planting, pruning, patching, dragging along never gaining never reaping never knowing and never understanding;

For my play mates in the clay and dust and sand of Alabama backyards playing, baptizing, and preaching and doctor and jail and soldier and school and store and hair and Miss Choomby and company;

For the cramped bewildered years we went to school to learn to know the reasons why and the answers to and the people who and the places where and the days when, in memory of the bitter hours when we discovered we were black and poor and small and different and nobody cared and nobody wondered and nobody understood;

For the boys and girls who grew in spite of these things to be man and woman, to laugh and dance and sing and play and drink their wine and religion and success, to marry their playmates and bear children and then die of consumption and anemia and lynching;

For my people thronging 47th Street in Chicago and Lenox Avenue in New York and Rampart Street in New Orleans, lost disinherited, dispossessed and happy people filling the cabarets and taverns and other people's pockets needing bread and shoes and milk and money and something—something all our own;

For my people walking blindly spreading joy, losing time being lazy, sleeping when hungry, shouting when burdened, drinking when hopeless, tired and shackled and tangled among ourselves by the unseen creatures who tower over us omnisciently and laugh;

For my people blundering and groping and floundering in the dark of churches and schools and clubs and societies, associations and councils and committees and conventions, distressed and disturbed and deceived and devoured by money-hungry glory-craving leeches, preyed on by facile force of state and fad and novelty, by false prophet and holy believer;

For my people standing, staring, trying to fashion a better way from confusion, from hypocrisy and misunderstanding, trying to fashion a world that will hold all the people, all the faces, all the Adams and Eves and their countless generations;

Let a new earth rise. Let another world be born. Let a bloody peace be written in the sky. Let a second generation full of courage issue forth; let a people loving freedom come to growth. Let a beauty full of healing and a strength of final clenching be the pulsing in our spirits and our blood. Let the martial songs be written, let the dirges disappear. Let a race of men now rise and take control.

NARRATOR

Teachers and professors on black college campuses wrote one act plays for theaters. The time and mood of this period did not provide many grand opportunities for blacks to pursue professional careers in the theater. However, blacks did play the traditional roles as servants, maids and butlers in movies and theaters.

Pause

In 1939, Hattie McDaniel won the Academy Award for her best supporting role in "Gone With the Wind." Black film companies had very little success in the field of motion picture production. There were some gradual changes for some black actors. Paul Robeson played the role of "Othello" in London, England.

Pause

In 1934, Fannie Hurst's "Imitation of Life" introduced Louise Beaver and Fredi Washington. Entertainers like Bill Robinson, Hazel Scott and Lena Horne were successful in securing contracts with major producers.

Pause

Harlem was literally owned and controlled by white millionaires. The Cotton Club was one such nightspot. Although located in Harlem, only whites attended this club. The entertainers were mostly light complexion blacks. The waiter and waitresses had dark complexions. Lena Horne was a frequent performer there. This was the beginning of her successful career in entertainment.

Stage decorated, depicting scenes/motif of the Cotton Club. Stage has from four to five tables to seat couples escorted in by an unctuous waiter. High fashion gowns and tuxedoes abound. Ladies enter as stylish models. Men use proper etiquette with them.

MASTER OF CEREMONY suavely dressed in a club-coordinated attire. A lively individual.

MASTER OF CEREMONY

Ladies and gentlemen! Good evening, and welcome to The Cotton Club in Harlem, New York, the cultural capital of the USA.

Pause

We bring to you the finest entertainment here in the swank sizzling showplace—The Cotton Club! Sit back, relax, and travel vicariously to those fantastic years of Harlem, the cultural haven of New York.

Pause

I want you to know we have the finest revue for you tonight. You have given yourself the treat of your life by coming out tonight. Let me just name a few of our stars who will perform for you this evening.

Drums in the background coordinating the MC's presentation.

MASTER OF CEREMONY

We have that great jazz player out of New Orleans, Louis "Satchmo" Armstrong. Take note of Harlem's own, Bill "Bojangles" Robinson. Swing to the beat of Count Basie, Duke Ellington and Cab Calloway.

Pause

And now for the star attraction this evening, we have the lovely, talented and that beautiful actress, the one and only, Ms. Lena Horne! Get your hands together to welcome Ms. Lena Horne as she sings that number one hit, "Summer Time."

LENA, dressed in a fabulous long gown, walks out graciously, teasing men at the tables as she makes her entrance.

MASTER OF CEREMONY

Meets her with open arms, kisses her hand

And now ladies and gentlemen,

Pause

Ms. Lena Horne!

LENA HORNE sings "Summer Time," walks through tables and flirts with men; women give a warning eye. Lena closes with her "Stormy Weather." She is the only person performing in the Cotton Club. Other names have performed earlier in the program.

MASTER OF CEREMONY

Give her a big round of applause.

NARRATOR

The Cotton Club was symbolic of the great Harlem Renaissance. Blacks excelled in classical music, too. R. Nathaniel Dett was recognized for his piano compositions and voice ensembles. William Dawson, a graduate of Tuskegee Institute, was instrumental in bringing fame to the Tuskegee Choir by popularizing Negro Spirituals. Dean Dixon earned an international reputation as the conductor of the American Youth Symphony Orchestra.

Pause

Ladies and gentlemen, this program was only a brief synopsis of the period in our history known as the "Black Renaissance," well depicted as the Harlem Renaissance. The awakening of black talent in Harlem encouraged black people throughout America to take pride in being black and to seek to develop the talents endowed them by God.

Pause

What about you? Are you developing your talents? Be it a teacher, a singer, a dancer, a poet, a writer, a musician. Each one of you has gifts. Try developing them! As you do, seek to encourage and support others in developing and using theirs in a positive way that helps make this a better society.

BLACKOUT

THE END

III. *The Montgomery Bus Boycott*

Cast of Characters

NARRATOR

ROSA PARKS

POLICEMAN

BUS DRIVER

TAX DRIVER

MARTIN L. KING, JR.

RALPH D. ABERNATHY

HELEN PETERSON

RAYMOND WILLIS

PAUL HARDY

WHITE MAN

SISTER GRACE

OLD LADY

ANNIE LOU

MARY LUCY

SISTER ANN

REPORTER/SECRETARY

LEONA MASON

CHARLES BOWMAN

CLAUDETTE WILLIAMS

JOANN WILSON

OLD MAN

Two or more roles may be played by one person

SCENE: Montgomery, Alabama

TIME: December 1, 1955

Rosa Parks, whose refusal to move to the back of a bus touched off the Montgomery Bus Boycott and the beginning of the civil rights movement, is fingerprinted by police Lt. D.H. Lackey in Montgomery, Ala., Feb. 22, 1956. She was among some 100 people charged with violating segregation laws. (AP Photo/Gene Herrick)

—*ACT I*—

Scene 1

SETTING: *Court Square in Montgomery, Alabama*
AT RISE: *On a public bus, whites are seated in the front and blacks are seated in the back.*

NARRATOR

The Cleveland Avenue bus stops at Court Square. A tired, attractive black woman enters the bus. She moves to the back of the bus to the designated section for black people. She was lucky! There was just one seat left in this section. The black woman walked to the fifth row of the bus and sat next to a black man.

ROSA PARKS enters crowded bus and sits down wearily.

NARRATOR

The bus driver's next stop is at the Empire Theater. Several white people board the bus. One white man can not find a seat.

BUS DRIVER

Looks in rear view mirror

Get up and give this man a seat!

NARRATOR

The four black people who sit in the fifth row do not respond. This is certainly an unusual day. For years, black people had obeyed the segregation laws without the slightest amount of resistance.

BUS DRIVER

Y'all better make it light on yourselves and let me have those seats!

A black man crosses over ROSA PARKS to relinquish his seat.

ROSA PARKS moves into the seat next to the window. Two black women across the aisle vacate their seats. ROSA remains in her seat.

WHITE MAN

Bus driver, will you ask this black woman to get up and give me this seat!

BUS DRIVER

Stops the bus, approaches ROSA PARKS

Let me have that seat or else I will call the police!

ROSA PARKS

Shrugs her shoulders in a negative manner and still refuses to give up her seat.

Go ahead and call them.

BUS DRIVER storms to the front of the bus and pulls the ratchet, leaves the bus to call the police.

NARRATOR

J. F. Blake, the bus driver, returns with two policemen.

ROSA PARKS is approached by two POLICEMEN.

POLICEMAN

Will you get up and give your seat to the man?

ROSA PARKS

Why do you push us around?

POLICEMAN

I don't know, but the law is the law and you are under arrest!

POLICEMAN snatches ROSA by the arm and removes her from the bus.

NARRATOR

For the crime of not giving up her seat to a white man, Mrs. Rosa Parks, a respected member of the black community, is taken to jail. There she is booked and fingerprinted by Deputy Sheriff D.H. Lackey of Montgomery, Alabama. She is charged with violating the City's segregation law. During the past year alone, five black women and two black children had been arrested for disobeying bus drivers. One man had been shot to death by a policeman for the same offense.

Pause

Mrs. Parks had served as secretary of the local branch of the NAACP. Mr. E. D. Nixon, head of the NAACP, heard of her arrest and quickly posts bail for her release. She is later convicted and fined $10 and cost, a total of $14. The arrest of Rosa Parks triggers the Montgomery Bus Boycott. News of her arrest spreads quickly through the black community like wild fire.

BLACKOUT

END OF SCENE

Act I, Scene 2

SETTING: *Montgomery, Organization of the Boycott and M.I.A. (Montgomery Improvement Association).*
AT RISE: *Angry CROWD of blacks, walking around humming, buzzing and talking.*

MRS. MASON
You know they took our neighbor, Mrs. Rosa Parks, to jail because she wouldn't give her seat to a white man!

MRS. PETERSON
Sho' a nice black sister. I hate that!

MR. BOWMAN
Just plain refused to give up her seat. She show got some guts in her trough!

MR. WILLIS
I don't blame her. We tired of our women being treated like they some working horses.

CROWD
Amen! Amen! Tell it like it is.

MR. HARDY
And I feel that if we pay our money to ride on a public bus, we should be able to keep our seats.

MRS. WILSON
I'm tired of giving up my seat to a white person after I've paid my money.

DR. KING appears before the CROWD.

Dr. King

I've got a plan! I said, black people, I have a plan!

Mr. Willis

Who are you?

Dr. King

I'm Martin Luther King, Jr. and I am concerned about what's going on today with our people. I don't think that black people ought to continue to accept segregation and second-class citizenship. I think we, as a people, can make a change in these segregation laws.

Mrs. Mason

Just how do you figure we can do that? We been segregated for more than a hundred years!

Crowd

Yeah, what kind of plan do you have?

Mr. Bowman

I say, let's hear his plan!

Dr. King

My brothers and sisters, this evening, I want to tell you that there is nothing like, UNITY. We've got to have some TOGETHERNESS. Then we can really organize a boycott against the buses in Montgomery, Alabama!

Sister Grace

What do you mean?

Dr. King

I mean *don't ride the buses!*

Mr. willis

Just how do you figure I'm gonna get to work?

Annie Lou

I've got to get to church!

Sister Ann

And I got to go shopping!

Dr. King

I am aware of your needs. We can organize to help ourselves. We can form car pools. People who own cars will share their cars.

Mr. Hardy

Do you think that this will really work?

Dr. King

Do you own a car?

Mr. Hardy

Yeah.

Dr. King

Are you willing to share your car for the cause?

Mr. Bowman

I will!

Mrs. Williams

My brother has a car. I'm sure he will share it!

Taxi Driver

I'm a taxi driver and I believe I can persuade some of the other black taxi drivers to lend you a hand. There are 18 black taxi stands with a total of 210 cars.

Dr. King

This is, indeed, a good showing this evening. Most of you know Rev. Abernathy, pastor of the first Baptist Church in this city. He will read to you a list of resolutions which we will present to the bus company and city officials. Come forward, Rev. Abernathy!

The two men shake hands as group applauds.

Rev. Abernathy

We are involved in a very important cause. There is a need for us to take a stand. This is the time for us to let white people know that we are not going to accept this second-class treatment. Brothers and sisters, we have a very important duty to perform! I say to you that we must unite for this cause. I have here a list of demands to be met before we end our boycott.

1) Black people will not ride the buses until a more courteous treatment by bus drivers is guaranteed!

CROWD

Amen, that's right. We want equal rights.

REV. ABERNATHY

2) All passengers are to be seated on a "first come, first served" basis.

3) We want black people from the back of the bus and white people from the front of the bus.

CROWD

Praise God, that's the truth!

REV. ABERNATHY

4) We want black bus drivers employed to drive largely black routes.

DR. KING

Thank you, Rev. Abernathy. All those who are ready to accept these demands will you please stand!

The majority stand. Two or three sit for a few seconds, then stand.

Just for a spirit of UNITY, I would like everyone to repeat after me:

The CROWD will repeat the words after DR. KING.

CROWD

I WILL NOT RIDE, THE PUBLIC BUSES, IN MONTGOMERY, ALABAMA, UNTIL THEY ARE, DESEGREGATED AND ALL PEOPLE, BLACK AND WHITE, ARE TREATED, ON A FIRST COME, FIRST SERVED BASIS.

DR. KING

Let us all join in and sing "We Shall Overcome" as we march out tonight.

NARRATOR

Instead of riding the buses, black people thumbed rides, shared their cars, rode mules, and some middle-aged people even walked as many as twelve (12) miles a day to keep from riding the bus. When black people learned that Mrs. Rosa Parks had been found guilty of disobeying the segregation law and fined $14, this gave them a greater incentive to boycott the buses.

END OF SCENE

Act I, Scene 3

SETTING: *The Boycott, Montgomery, Alabama*
AT RISE: *BOYCOTTERS carried signs: "Don't Ride the Buses," "First come, First served," "End Segregation," "First-class Citizenship Now," and "Remember Rosa Parks!"*

DR. KING holds up a sign and stops with a firm stand and speaks in an authoritative voice.

DR. KING

Don't ride the buses!

REV. ABERNATHY holds up a sign and speaks in a demanding tone.

REV. ABERNATHY

First come, first served!

BOYCOTTER #3

Holds up a sign and speaks in an assertive tone.

Don't discriminate!

BOYCOTTER #4

Holds up a sign and speaks in a warning tone.

God made us all!

BOYCOTTER #5

Holds up a sign and speaks in a chastising tone.

First-class citizenship, now!

BOYCOTTER #6

Holds up a sign and speaks in a tone as if charging people with a mission.

And remember Rosa Parks!

The BOYCOTTERS resound the words by chanting in a high tone of voice and then in a low tone: "Remember Rosa Parks" as they march around in a circle until curtains are closed.

BLACKOUT

END OF SCENE

Act I, Scene 4

SETTING: *The old woman's walk.*
AT RISE: *An old woman dressed in a hat, wearing eyeglasses, leaning on a cane, possibly carrying a shoulder pocketbook.*

NARRATOR

Some people preferred to walk, feeling that it was a symbolic act in the struggle for justice. One driver stopped alongside an elderly black woman who was slowly making her way down the street.

TAXI DRIVER slows down the car and speaks in a respectful tone of voice.

TAXI DRIVER

Lady, let me give you a ride. You don't have to walk!

OLD WOMAN looks up slowly with her hand trembling on her cane and makes her point for walking.

OLD WOMAN

I'm not walking for myself, sonny. I'm walking for my children and my grandchildren!

Curtains remain open until OLD WOMAN has walked across the stage.

BLACKOUT

END OF ACT I

—ACT II—

Scene 1

SETTING: *Office of the M.I.A.*
AT RISE: *A secretary is seated at a desk with a telephone. DR. KING and REV. ABERNATHY are seated at a desk. REV. ABERNATHY holds up an envelope and responds.*

REV. ABERNATHY
We have received contributions from churches in practically every city in the United States.

DR. KING
We haven't done too badly with contributions from other countries. Here are checks from Tokyo, from Singapore and from Switzerland.

NARRATOR
The boycott was hard work. It was also expensive. It took $5,000 a month to run the car pool. Rich people and poor people supported the boycott in Montgomery. Then they began receiving support from all over the world.

REV. ABERNATHY
Listen to this note of encouragement. "Your work is outstanding in the history of our country."
Pause
"You have shown that decency and courage will eventually prevail."

DR. KING
Here is one note I would like to believe. It says, "The entire nation salutes you."

NARRATOR
The work increased for the leaders, Dr. King and Rev. Abernathy, but they refused to give up. Threats are made by whites on Dr. King's life.

BLACKOUT

END OF SCENE

Act II, Scene 2

SETTING: *Threatening phone call at DR. MARTIN L. KING, JR.'s home.*

AT RISE: *DR. KING is sleeping. Telephone rings. Dressed in house robe, he answers the telephone.*

WHITE VOICE

Listen, nigger, we've taken all we want from you. Before next week you'll be sorry you ever came to Montgomery, Alabama!

DR. KING hangs up the telephone nervously.

MRS. KING is dressed in house robe. She carries a cup of coffee in her hand. She walks over to DR. KING and gives him a gentle pat on the back.

MRS. KING

Don't worry, Martin. God is with you!

DR. KING falls on bended knees in prayer. Remains until curtains are closed.

NARRATOR

Dr. King found inner strength from prayer. When times were too hard for him, he prayed. When it seemed as if he had been drained of courage, he quickly revived himself through prayer. He couldn't afford to show his fear. There were too many people who looked to him for leadership.

BLACKOUT

END OF SCENE

Act II, Scene 3

SETTING: *The bombing of DR. MARTIN L. KING, JR's home.*

AT RISE: *MRS. KING and a church member, MARY LUCY, are watching television. They hear a loud noise*

NARRATOR

The Boycott is successful, but there are still bitter days ahead. Three days later while Mrs. King and a church member, Mary Lucy, are watching television, something strange happens. Mrs. King's nine-week old daughter, Yoki, is asleep in the back room of the house.

Pause

Without warning, a loud noise is heard.

Pause

Quickly, they rush to the back part of the house to check on the baby. Suddenly, the bomb explodes, shattering windows and sending smoke into the room.

Pause

Mary Lucy tries to comfort Mrs. King.

Pause

There is heavy knocking at Mrs. King's door.

MRS. KING opens door.

Neighbors rush in to help. Luckily, no one is injured.

Pause

Later, Mrs. King's telephone rings.

Telephone rings three times. MRS. KING finds her way to the telephone and picked up the receiver.

It is the voice of a woman who said:

VOICE

Behind curtain

"Yes, I did it! I'm sorry I didn't kill all of you!"

BLACKOUT

END OF SCENE

Act II, Scene 4

Setting: *Montogmery, Alabama. Angry mob and the non-violent crusader.*

At Rise: *A group of blacks talked loudly about what they were going to do to retaliate and many of them openly carried a variety of weapons.*

Narrator

A large number of blacks armed themselves with guns, rocks, bats, knives, sticks and bottles. After he received the distressful news, Dr. King returned to his home, and made his way through the crowd. He was relieved when he found that his family was safe and kissed his wife and baby.

Pause

After seeing to his family, Dr. King went outside to try to calm down the angry crowd.

Crowd is reluctant to put down weapons.

Dr. King

We are tired of being segregated and humiliated! We are impatient for justice. But we will protest with love. There will be no cross burnings. No white person will be taken from his home by a hooded Negro mob and murdered. If we do this, if we protest with love, future historians will have to say, there lived a great people, a black people who injected new meaning and dignity into the veins of civilization. I believe in nonviolence. Get rid of your weapons. We must love our white brothers no matter what they do to us. What we are doing is just and God is with us!

Tense and angry faces disappear slowly. Weapons are dropped two by two. The Crowd begins to disperse.

Old Man walks up to Dr. King.

Old Man

God bless you, son!

Narrator

To show their anger about the political action by blacks, the City of Montgomery began arresting some of the most respected blacks in the city. They were accused of conspiring to destroy business in Montgomery.

The first to be tried was Dr. King. He was found guilty and fined $500. Newspapers throughout the country carry these stories and put the spotlight on the injustices found in Montgomery, Alabama.

BLACKOUT

END OF SCENE

Act II, Scene 5

SETTING: *Victory for the M.I.A. office in Montgomery, Alabama.*
AT RISE: *DR. KING and REV. ABERNATHY and other workers at the M.I.A. office.*

NARRATOR

Finally, Dr. King and the M.I.A. received a response from the United States Federal District Court. This court learned that the City's bus suit would not stop there. The Boycotters took the case to the United States Supreme Court in Washington, D.C.

Pause

It was a long wait. By November, the spirits of blacks were very low. For in the meantime, the City of Montgomery was still trying to destroy their boycott. But at the right time, Dr. King and the boycotters received good news.

REPORTER rushes in with good news.

REPORTER

Look, Dr. King, here's a news release! The United States Supreme Court has ruled in your favor!

DR. KING

Reads the release from the newspaper

Alabama State and local laws requiring segregation on buses unconstitutional!

M.I.A. CROWD rushes in to the good news.

M.I.A. Crowd

Jubilee! Thank God! We won! We won!

Dr. King

Let us bow our heads to give a word of thanks.

BLACKOUT

Narrator

The united blacks under the leadership of Dr. King won their fight.

Pause

On December 21, 1956, Dr. Martin Luther King got on the South Jackson Street bus and took a seat next to the window. Reverend Glenn Smiley, a white minister from New York, got on and sat down next to Dr. King. White man and black man, side by side, in Montgomery, Alabama went for a ride on the bus.

Pause

The bus boycott lasted 381 days until blacks had won their rights and demands.

BLACKOUT

THE END

I AM ONLY ONE PERSON

Anonymous

I am only one person. What can one person do?
Rosa Parks was just one person.
She said one word. She said it on December 1, 1955.

One person said one word.
She said it on a bus. She said it to a bus driver
On the Cleveland Street Bus in Montgomery

The bus driver said, "Stand up, [Black Woman],
And give your seat to that white man!"

Rosa Parks, one person, said one word.
The word was "NO!"

One woman said one word and a nation blushed.
One woman said one word and a world talked.
One woman said one word and the Supreme Court acted.
One woman said one word and the buses desegregated.

I am only one person what can one person do?

They put her in jail because she "didn't know her place."
Because she didn't "stay in her place"
Because she was an uppity [Black Woman].

It was a Thursday when she said that one word.
On Monday morning the buses ran.
The Negroes walked.
Each white had two seats. Empty seats,
Symbols of a people moved to walk, moved to march, moved to act
By the sound of one woman's, "NO!"

One woman said one word and 17,000 people walked.

He was a Nobel Prize winner whose life was notably without lacking in peace. As an embattled young minister he once owned a gun but got rid of it because to him possessing the weapon symbolized not defense but his own spiritual death.

He was an advocate of brotherhood who was jailed repeatedly, kicked, spat on, stabbed nearly to death and finally murdered.

The terrible paradox of his life was summed up in his death: his search for a nonviolent solution to racial problems placed him squarely between the advocates of violence on both sides of the racial struggle. Vilified by blacks who saw his nonviolence as weakness, feared by whites who felt threatened because his methods were so effective, he knew his middle position was dangerous.

It all came about because of the aching feet of a Black woman.
In the early evening of Thursday, December 1, 1955, a Montgomery City Lines bus rolled through Court Square and headed for its next stop.

Aboard were 24 Black people seated from the rear toward the front, and 12 whites, seated from front to back. At the Empire Theatre stop six Whites boarded the bus.

The driver, as usual, walked back and asked the foremost Black person to get up so the Whites could sit. Three Black people obeyed, but Mrs. Rosa Parks, a seamstress who had once been a local secretary for the National Association for the Advancement of Colored People, did the unexpected. She refused.

"I don't know why I wouldn't move," said Rosa Parks.
"There was no plot or plan at all. I was tired from shopping. My feet hurt." Rosa Parks was arrested and fined $10 and costs for violating a law requiring bus passengers to follow drivers' seating assignments.

Overnight the word flashed throughout the various Black neighborhoods. Support Rosa Parks **DON'T RIDE THE BUSES** on Monday, December 1, 1955.

Within 48 hours mimeographed leaflets had been distributed calling for a one-day bus boycott. The results were astonishing. On Monday Montgomery Black People walked, rode mules, drove horse-drawn buggies and traveled to work in private cars.

The Bus Boycott was 90% effective. Blacks in Montgomery held this boycott for 381 days, until the buses were desegregated and all passengers were received on a first-come, first-served basis.

What can one person do? One person can turn a nation around!

IV. *The Negro Mother*

THE NEGRO MOTHER

Anonymous

Children, I come back today,
To tell you a story of the long dark way
That I had to climb, that I had to know,
In order that the race might live and grow.
Look at my face—dark as the night—
Yet shining as the sun with loves true light. *"The Heritage"*

I am the child they stole from the sand
Three hundred years ago from Africa's land,
I am the dark girl who crossed the wide sea
Carrying in my body the seed of the Free.
I am the woman who worked in the field
Bringing the cotton and the corn to yield! *"The Bondage"*
I am the one who labored as a slave
Beaten and mistreated for the work that I gave,
Children sold away from me, husband sold, too
No safety, no respect was I due
But God put a song and a prayer in my heart.
I would bear my burden and do my part.

Now through my children, young and free
I realize the blessing denied to me.
I couldn't read then, and I couldn't write. *"The Hope"*
I had nothin', back there in the dark, dark night.
Sometimes, the valley was filled with tears.
But, I had to keep trudging on through the lonely years.
Sometimes, the road was hot with the sun,
Nothin' could stop me, I kept on goin'.

I had to keep goin', no stopping for me,
I was the seed of the coming free,
I nourished the dream that nothing could smother,
Deep in my breast—The Negro Mother—
I had only hope then, but now through you,
Dark ones of today, my dreams must come true. *"The Persistence"*
Remember my years, a torch for tomorrow
Make of my past, a road to the light
Out of the darkness, the ignorance, the night.

Lift my banner, out of the dust
Stand tall like free men, supporting my trust.
Believe in the right, let none push you back
Remember the whip and the slaver's track.

"The Dream"

Remember how the strong in struggle and strife
Still bar your way, to deny you life
But marching ever forward, breaking down bars
Look ever upward, at the sun and the stars.
Oh, my dark children, may my dreams and prayers
Impel you forever up the stairs—
For I will be with you 'til no white brother
Dares keep down the children of, THE NEGRO MOTHER.

THE NEGRO MOTHER

Rendition for "Grandma Emma"
A Dramatic Choreography by Dorothy Swygert

SPIRIT OF MOTHER AFRICA *(Free and flowing with history and truth)*

THE HERITAGE

THE NEGRO MOTHER: Children, I come back today,
To tell you a story of the long dark way
That I had to climb, that I had to know,
In order that the race might live and grow.

Points to face and extends right hand upward—bright light shines

Look at my face—dark as the night
Yet shining as the sun with loves true light!

AFRICAN DRUMS: *Drummers in background dressed in African attire; African dancers with soft, light rhythm serenade through with flowing African cloth.*

THE BONDAGE

THE NEGRO MOTHER: I am the child they stole from the sand three hundred years ago from Africa's land.

AFRICAN DRUMS: *A heavy long beat by the drummers with majestic music—from ascending to descending sounds—ending in a soft beat.*

THE NEGRO MOTHER: I am the dark girl who crossed the wide sea
Carrying in my body, the SEED of the FREE.

AFRICAN DRUMS: *Low, rhythmic rising beat.*

PLANTATION SCENE: *Slaves bent over with cotton sacks, toiling in the background as the NEGRO MOTHER continues to speak.*

THE NEGRO MOTHER: I AM THE WOMAN who worked in the field
Bringing the cotton and the corn to yield!

PLANTATION OVERSEER: *Enters field with a long lash, screaming at the slaves and beating them with the lash.*

THE NEGRO MOTHER: I am the one who LABORED AS A SLAVE
Beaten and mistreated for the work I gave.

SLAVE QUARTET: *Dressed in long sack cloth gowns with head dress with sad countenance singing, "Go Down Moses."*

AUCTION BLOCK SCENE: *Big strong male slave on the elevated auction block in shackles, with a line-up of children and more slaves.*

THE NEGRO MOTHER: *Tears in her eyes, sorrowful countenance, gazing in the sky.*
Children sold away from me, husband sold, too,
no safety, no respect was I due.

SLAVE OVERSEER: *Motions with hands to the Negro Mother, beckoning her to his quarters.*

AFRICAN DRUMS: *Medium high rhythmic beat*

THE NEGRO MOTHER: *Return to stage*
But God put a song and a prayer in my heart,
I would bear my burden and do my part.
She bows on her knees in prayerful position.

SLAVE QUARTET: *From bending knee position, the SLAVE QUARTET begins singing, "Steal Away to Jesus".*

THE HOPE

THE NEGRO MOTHER: *A smile and an expression hope on her face.*
Now through my children, young and free,
I realize the blessings denied me.

FREEDOM DANCERS: *Young girls in circle, dressed in freedom colors, joyfully dance around in circle and spread out with out stretched hands.*

INTERLUDE

THE NEGRO MOTHER: I couldn't read then, and I couldn't write
I had nothing back there, in the dark, dark night.

Sometimes the valley was filled with tears
But, I had to keep trudging on through the lonely hard years.

Hands clenched to her breast, with a solemn facial expression.
Sometimes the road was hot with the sun,
Nothin' could stop me, I kept goin' on.

THE PERSISTENCE

THE NEGRO MOTHER: I had to keep goin', no stopping for me,
I was the seed of the coming free.

With arms affectionately resting across her breast

I nourished the dream that nothing could smother,
Deep in my breast—The Negro Mother!

AFRICAN DRUMMERS: *Give three loud high rising chords*

FREEDOM DANCERS: *Quiet rhythmic dance portraying the aged mother of wisdom*

THE NEGRO MOTHER: *Looks at audience as with a command.*
I had only HOPE then, but now through you
points to audience
Dark ones of today, my dreams must come true!

An austere charge
Remember my years, heavy with sorrow
And make of those years, a torch for tomorrow!

FREEDOM DANCERS: *Rise up from background of a circle and emerge with a torch.*

Make of my past, a road to the light
Out of the DARKNESS, the ignorance, the night.

THE DREAM

FREEDOM DANCERS: *On floor, bend back and forth, then emerge with a banner.*

THE CHALLENGE

THE NEGRO MOTHER: Lift high my banner, out of the dust,
Stand tall like FREE MEN, supporting my TRUST.

THE SPIRIT OF TRUTH

THE NEGRO MOTHER: Believe in the right, let none push you back
Remember the whip and the slaver's track

Remember how the strong in struggle and strife
Still bar your way, and deny you life

Reaches in pocket and pulls out eyeglasses and with the stern appearance of a Sunday school teacher, she continues to speak.

THE ADHERING CROWD: *Young men, young women, young children emerge on stage.*

THE NEGRO MOTHER: *Looks at the emerging group and bows her head with assurance.*

But marching ever forward, breaking down bars
Look ever upward, at the sun and the
Stars.

Looks up as to heaven with Bible in her hands and then at the group

Oh, my dark children, may my dreams and
prayers
Impel you forever up the stairs—

STAIR BLOCK: *Men of different professions ascend the stairs and take a strong authoritative stand.*

For I will be with you 'til no white brother
Dares keep down the children of
THE NEGRO MOTHER!

v. The Reunion

Cast of Characters

GRANVILLE:	Air Force Officer
ANN:	Granville's college sweetheart
GEORGE:	Classmate and war friend
JEAN:	Granville's wife
BARBARA:	George's wife

THEME: Romance, Relationships and Reasoning

SCENE: College Campus

TIME: Fall '84

—ACT I—

Scene 1

Setting: *College Campus in Douglass Guest Hall.*

At Rise: *Granville, a tall, slender forty-one-year old man is in his room in Douglass Guest Hall on the college campus. This is his first day on campus. He arrived last night for the Homecoming Reunion. He decided to sleep late. It is still morning, and he is up staring out the window. As he stands with his hands resting on his waist, twenty years rush quickly before him.*

The ROTC (Reserved Officers' Training Corps) Training Hall is visible.

Granville

A pleasant expression appears on his face.

There are the hills and valleys, the trees and the landscaped grounds. This campus has been known for its beauty through the years.

Moves his right arm from his waist and cups it on his chin.

I remember the day when our country received the most dolorous news of the century: President John F. Kennedy was assassinated. All of the students on campus were sad.

Pause

I remember the day very well. I went to the girls' dorm to pick up Ann to escort her to the chapel.

A stern expression appears on his face.

We attended the memorial service for our beloved President.

Shakes his head in awe. Suddenly, a gleam appeared in his eyes for a moment.

Ann, Ann, Ann!

Shakes his head.

It's so strange how the future unfolds right before your eyes, as if you have no control.

A remorseful expression appears on his face as if he were looking back into the past.

How I remember those early mornings of ROTC training with the Air Force!

Bows his head in affirmative.

Just to think that I've been in the Air Force for a total of twenty years and three of those years were spent on this campus.

Smiles

Recognition?

Pause

Yes, I suppose I have had a decent share of it!

Off: A knock on the door.

Yes?

VOICE

Room service!

GRANVILLE turns away from the window and walks to the door, opens it. Bows a good morning to the WAITER.

WAITER

Points to tray

Did you order this?

GRANVILLE

Looks down at tray

Yes, I sure did order coffee and a newspaper.

GRANVILLE holds the door open.

Just bring it right in.

WAITER

Rolls tray into room.

Where do you want this?

GRANVILLE

Right over there will be just fine.

Bows head in approval.

Thank you!

Pays WAITER.

WAITER

Takes money

Thank you. Have a good day, sir!

GRANVILLE

Same to you.

GRANVILLE closes the door. He pours a cup of coffee and sits at the table near the window to admire the campus side view.
His thoughts are overcoming him. Before he knows it, he finds himself in a campus soliloquy.

GRANVILLE

Yes, yes, it's really a good feeling to be back here on campus.

As he is about to pour his second cup of coffee, there is a knock on the door.
Pauses, places coffee pot on table without pouring his coffee. Ponders who could be at the door.

GRANVILLE

Calls out

Who is it?

VOICE

Responds

George.

Pause

Your old dorm pal!

GRANVILLE gets up quickly and moves to the door and opens it.
GEORGE hands extended openly, a big smile on his face.

GEORGE

What is this? You must think that you're still in Vietnam!

Both men laugh and chuckle.

GRANVILLE

Grabs him by right hand and pulls him in

Just come on in and stop the BS-ing!

GEORGE

Stands back, tall and straight

How long has it been since we were together in Viet Fields?

He gesticulates with left hand as if making a count.

GRANVILLE

Stands back looking GEORGE up and down

I can't believe it!

Places left hand on waist with right hand cupping his chin.

Son-of-a-gun!

Both men laugh and embrace again.

GEORGE

Sits in chair opposite GRANVILLE's cup

I checked in yesterday morning.

GRANVILLE

Shakes head as if still in amazement

You did!

GEORGE

Clapping both hands on his knees

I ran into old Kleever…

GRANVILLE

Picks up sentence before GEORGE finishes

In engineering?

GEORGE

Yeah.

Smiles

And he told me that you had checked in last night.

GRANVILLE hits right hand on table. Both men laugh out loudly, filled with joy.

GEORGE

Smile disappears, serious expression appears

Yes, it is good seeing you, Gran.

Pause

It's been about twelve years since we were together in Vietnam.

GRANVILLE

Serious expression appears

Time stands still for no man.

Pause

I thought we would never get out of the "fields" alive.

Crosses his right leg over his left leg and braces it with his left hand.

GEORGE

Solemn expression. Speaks slowly.

Whenever I think of Vietnam… I think of you. I will never forget how we were in that trap and you figured out a plan for us to get out!

GRANVILLE

Serious expression. Speaks thoughtfully.

It's all about teamwork. We were good at working together.

GEORGE

You know, Gran… I often think of how lucky we were to get back to the States alive!

GRANVILLE

Shakes head quickly as if erasing the pain of the war away

Yeah.

Pause

I don't like to think about the number of classmates who were killed in that war.

GEORGE

Stands and looks out the window

It's as if it were just a few years ago when we were running over to the ROTC Training Hall for training.

GRANVILLE

Well, that war is hard to sum up.

Pause

I guess if you were to sum it up, you would say that it was, "A WAR THAT COULDN'T BE WON!"

GEORGE

Changes subject, looks at GRANVILLE

Well, I see that you haven't earned your beer gut.

Both men laugh.

You're still as tall and slim as you were.

Chuckles

Remember when!

GRANVILLE

And you haven't done too badly, yourself.
How do you keep it?

GEORGE

Smiles

Since "Nam," I've been basically occupied with running my own business!

GRANVILLE

Gleam of approval appears in his eyes

Hey, hey, hey. Now that's great!

GEORGE

Yeah. I have my own chemical laboratory!

GRANVILLE

Bows head with a solemn look of approval

You were always interested in science!

GEORGE

Barbara, the kids and I have been in Cincinnati since I received my discharge.

GRANVILLE

Did they come with you?

GEORGE

Yes, they're out touring the campus.

Pause

What about you, Gran? What are you doing now? You were always great in engineering!

GRANVILLE

Props his legs on a chair

In spite of our days in Vietnam, I've remained with the Air Force.

GEORGE

So, you've made a career out of it?

GRANVILLE

Yes, yes, you can say that.

Laughs; looks at George

Twenty years under my belt now! After Vietnam, I served as an instructor on campus for two years. From there I took an assignment in Texas.

GEORGE

The Longhorn State! How long were you there?

GRANVILLE

Smiles

Oh…

Holds head back as if to recall by count.

Just about five years!

GEORGE

Eagerly catching up on the past

I bet you got a promotion.

GRANVILLE chuckles

GEORGE

Come on, Gran, tell it to me straight!

GRANVILLE

Chuckles

Of course I got a promotion!

GEORGE

Laughs

And you're…

Pause

Major!

GRANVILLE smiles

GEORGE stands up and gives GRANVILLE a military salute

Congratulations, man.
You really deserve it.

GRANVILLE bows head in military acceptance. Then both men smile. GRANVILLE sits down.

GRANVILLE

After Texas, I received my present assignment. I'm working…

George

Don't tell me! I know it has something to do with engineering.

Granville

I'm working with electronics security.

George

Laughs and slaps an approval on his hands

I knew it! Where are you stationed?

Granville

Maryland. Right in capitol zone.

George

Andrews Air Force Base?

Looks up at Granville.

Granville

Bows head in affirmative

That's right!

George

Smile fades into a serious expression

You and Jean are still together?

Granville

Bows his head slowly

Yes, Jean and I are still together.

Silence

George

Listens attentively

You had two children when you were in Vietnam.

Granville

Serious expression

And I have four boys now.

George

Speaks in cautious, counseling tone

There was someone you were very fond of in college.

Pause

You mentioned her name several times in the fields of Vietnam.

GRANVILLE gets up and stands in the window. Speaks in a remorseful tone.

GRANVILLE

It's been twenty years now.

GEORGE

You still carry those secret feelings for her. Don't you?

GRANVILLE

Still looking out the window, pensively.

I guess there are some things… All of us carry closely in our hearts… Sometimes in life. And I, being no exception, am guilty, too.

GEORGE

In an understanding but challenging tone.

In all those years…

Pause

You haven't seen her?

Looks up at GRANVILLE for an answer.

GRANVILLE

Serious tone

In all of those years…

Pause

No, I haven't seen her.

GEORGE

But those feelings?

Pause

All of those years!

Pause

You haven't seen her.

Pause

But she's been with you?

GRANVILLE bows head in the affirmative.

GEORGE gets up and walks over to the window, pats him on the back.

GEORGE

Oh, pal.

Shakes his head.

The torch is burning after twenty years!

GRANVILLE

In a pensive mood

I've learned to cover the torch...

Pause

so that I can get through life's tasks.

Pause

But I haven't quite learned how to extinguish it.

GEORGE walks back to his seat. GRANVILLE is still standing in the window.

GEORGE

Silence for a few moments, then slowly

The greatest virtues I've heard of...were nature, patience, and time.

GRANVILLE

Serious tone, pleading for an answer

Haven't I faced all three?

GEORGE

Then... Maybe your problem is solved!

GRANVILLE

Speaks in an unsatisfactory tone

Then why am I still blind to this?

GEORGE

Maybe you will just have to see uh, uh, what's her name? Don't tell me!

Rubs right hand across his forehead.

It's uh... Ann.

GRANVILLE

Sits down in a pensive mood

See her?

GEORGE

Yes. See her!

GRANVILLE

That's the problem!

GEORGE

Don't look at it like that. Put your request into the universe, and you might just be surprised.

Looks at his watch.

Oh, it's getting towards one o'clock. I told Barbara and the kids that I would meet them at the museum.

GRANVILLE

Changes the subject

Oh, by the way, how do you think the football game will go?

GEORGE

Standing near table

Well, they have a pretty good record this year.

Pause

You know, Bowie, who graduated with our class, is back as coach now!

GRANVILLE

AM "U" has a good record, too! At least, that's what I've been told.

Both men laugh loudly

But we'll both be there tomorrow to cheer the Golden Tigers to victory!

GEORGE

Walks toward the door

That's one thing about us. We still have that good old school spirit!

Both men laugh.

GEORGE opens the door to exit.

Oh, by the way…

Pauses in door and winks his left eye.

I heard that this is the largest return of graduates in its history!

GRANVILLE smiles as if picking up a message.

GEORGE

Happy mood

See ya at the football game!

GRANVILLE

You bet!

GRANVILLE closes the door, returns to his chair for a few moments, reflecting on the conversation. Stands and gazes out the window.

GRANVILLE

How time does pass! Well, let me get dressed and get ready for today's schedule.

BLACKOUT

END OF SCENE

Act I, Scene 2

SETTING: *Lobby of Douglass Guest Hall*
AT RISE: *GRANVILLE enters the lobby, overwhelmed and cannot believe his eyes. A very attractive LADY is talking on the telephone in the lobby. She's wearing a white custom-fitted suit, a yellow silk blouse with an open collar exposing a tri-color gold chain around her neck and a pair of black and white sling back pumps. Immediately, GRANVILLE stops in his tracks. He's eager to rush up to her but is afraid that it may not be the person he is thinking about. He makes a step forward, pauses, then moves backward. And before he can make up his mind to inquire, the LADY turns around. The LADY and GRANVILLE both freeze.*

GRANVILLE

Ann?

ANN drops the telephone receiver. They rush into each other's arm ecstatically.

GRANVILLE holds Ann's hands—stretched out so he can get a full view.

GRANVILLE

Ann, you're still as beautiful as ever. I had no problem recognizing you with your back turned.

ANN

Looking up at him

And you, you're as tall, slender, and handsome as I remember you.

Still holding hands, she smiles.

I was just making a call to confirm a flight to Washington, D.C. I have a conference to attend.

They drop hands.

GRANVILLE

Concerned expression

When do you leave?

ANN

I have a late flight out tomorrow night.

GRANVILLE

Sigh of relief

It's been a long time!

ANN looks down, as the smile disappears, then looks up into his face.

ANN

Yes.

Pause

It's been twenty years exactly.

GRANVILLE

Shakes his head

Where does time go?

A familiarity of bygone years begins to reflect on their faces.

ANN

A place where the memories are forbidden to travel.

GRANVILLE

Serious expression overcome by a smile to disguise the thoughts of the past

Why are we standing here? Let's go into the lounge and close the gap on those twenty years!

They walk in silence, each immersed in their own memories.

GRANVILLE pulls the chair out for her and adjusts it. He sits down.

ANN

Are you still in the Air Force?

GRANVILLE

Yes, I am. I guess I knew I would always make a career of it.

Smiles; points to the concession area.

Would you like something?

Ann

Smiles

No, I just finished a late breakfast.

Looks up at Granville

Tell me more about yourself.

Granville

Rests elbows on the table

Well…

Pause

I've traveled quite a bit since I've been in the Air Force.

Ann

Inquisitiveness

What places?

Granville

Beginning to soften, to surrender the heart

We traveled through most of Europe and Asia.

Ann

We?

Pauses for an answer

Granville

Gives quick eye contact

Yes. I mean, the family did some traveling with me, too!

Ann

Continues inquiry

You're still together?

Pauses for an answer.

Granville

A discerning look appears on his face as he nods his head

Yes. We're still together.

Silence

And you?

Ann looks down at her ring and both begin to smile. Ann stops smiling and looks up at Granville.

ANN

Yes, I am married. We've been married for fifteen years.

GRANVILLE

Inquisitive

Someone you met on the East Coast?

ANN

Yes, but actually, we were communicating during my last year of college. I just took some time for myself before deciding to marry.

GRANVILLE

Smiles and places right hand under his chin

I guess that's part of the liberation movement with women!

ANN

Half smile reverts to serious mood. Looks up at GRANVILLE

Well, no.

Pause

There were some things I had to clear from my head before marriage.

GRANVILLE

Digressive

Do you have any children?

ANN

Holds up two fingers of her right hand

Boys.

Pause

One's six and the other is thirteen.

GRANVILLE

Smiles

Well, we still have something in common.

ANN looks up with an expression which asks what?

GRANVILLE smiles

We both have boys only!

ANN

Laughs

Why, you're a chauvinistic male.

They clinch hands in their laughter.

GRANVILLE

Looks at her hands, then kisses them; Serious expression appears on his face

It's been a long time, Ann, twenty years since we've seen each other. Time has passed, but I must be honest with you. Despite the time gap, nothing happened to the feelings I've always had for you.

GRANVILLE gets up, takes her hand and they walk towards the window.

Yes, I've traveled all over the world and pursued a career in the Air Force. I'm still married to Jean and I have four sons.

Pause

But nothing could ever replace the feelings in my heart for you.

He looks down into ANN's eyes.

I never forgot you.

GRANVILLE's holding both of her hands.

ANN

I guess that's why it took me so long to decide to get married.

GRANVILLE

What do you mean?

ANN

It was difficult for me to try to reach out to someone else when my feelings were still with you.

GRANVILLE

The first years of my marriage were very trying!

ANN

Oh?

GRANVILLE

Yes! Those were the years when you were so much with me but not with me.

He looks at ANN.

Do you understand?

ANN

Looks puzzled

Go on.

GRANVILLE

In spite of everything that happened, I could only think of you.

Pause

I think I may have mentioned it to you on campus.

GRANVILLE pulls up two chairs to the window.

ANN

Solemn expression

Yes, I remember. I think I had just left the dining hall after lunch.

Pause

And you stopped me.

GRANVILLE

Serious expression

During that time, you were trying to avoid me.

ANN

I remember you telling me that you and Jean were constantly having fights.

GRANVILLE

And the fights were always about you!

ANN

I could not really relate to that at that time.

Pause

It took all of my being to heal my own wounds.

GRANVILLE crosses his arms and sits back in chair.

Well?

GRANVILLE

Smiles

It was hard making the adjustment.

Pause

I'd always imagined myself being married to you.

ANN

Evasive. Looks out the window and smiles

Gran, do you remember that tree down in the valley?

GRANVILLE

Looks out the window and smiles

How could I forget?

Smiles

That was our favorite spot after eating supper in the dining hall.

ANN

And there's Washington Hall! I remember the night I had to…

GRANVILLE

Spend the night in Steven's Hall because you were locked out of Washington Hall.

They both laugh.

ANN

Excitement in voice

I was so afraid I wouldn't get in!

GRANVILLE

Serious expression

That was the night we went to the Chapel for President Kennedy's memorial service.

Silence

After that we went for a ride to sit by the lake.

Smiles

Our favorite spot!

ANN

Smiles

We walked and talked and before we knew it…

Pause

It was late.

GRANVILLE

So late, until you were locked out of your dormitory.

They laugh.

Wow! I was in trouble!

ANN

Right! You were in serious trouble!

GRANVILLE

I kept trying to find a solution. I suggested that you spend the night off campus with my aunt.

ANN

Retorts humorously

The nerves!

Smile

I was too innocent to do that!

GRANVILLE

You were concerned about what my aunt would think of you.

Pause

And I was worried about where you were going to sleep that night.

ANN

Jovial tone

Well, we finally found a door that was still open.

GRANVILLE

You were lucky. You found your home girl living in the dorm.

ANN

Yes, she saved the night for me. Early that morning I slipped back into my dorm without the "house mother" missing me.

Serious expression

Otherwise, I would have had to face the Council and probably put on probation.

GRANVILLE

Smiles

I still remember your lakeside shake.

ANN

Vanilla, of course!

They laugh.

GRANVILLE

Looks up at ANN—serious expression

You've been with me through the years, although you were not with me.

Ann

Glances out window, then looks at Granville

Time has a way with the heart.

Granville

Continues in a serious tone

You know I was in the service throughout the Vietnam War.

Ann

I read in the Campus Newspaper that you were awarded a medal in 1971 for meritorious service.

Smiles

I was so proud of you.

Looks at him

Granville

I mentioned Vietnam, just to say that you were with me there, too! We were constantly faced with death traps and under fire weapons. But within my heart, I carried the sweet memories of you and the love that developed so quickly and ended too soon.

Silence

Somehow, it seemed as if just the thought of you, helped to increase my will power and gave me the determination to endure the battles of the war.

Ann

Serious expression

Gran, I thought I could live with the decision I made to you…

Pause

…that June of '64 but I have to be honest with you.

Pause

that decision did not represent the real me. It haunted me for years to come. I guess that's why I waited several years after college before deciding to get married.

Granville

Glares out the window and over the valley

It's awfully funny how it seems as if we have no control over our destiny! President Kennedy was assassinated.

Pause

And as we attended the memorial service together so in love, we had no idea that we were spending our last few weeks together before the break-off.

Ann

Digressing. Solemn expression turns into a smile

We had so many good times together.

Granville

Warm response

Very good memories! I guess if I were trying to identify the best time, I would have a problem trying to do so!

Ann

Looks up at Granville

A time that is most prominent in my memories is when you called me on the telephone to invite me to the Alpha Fraternity Ball.

A glimmer appears in her eyes.

Granville

His smile indicates a regression to that period

We had been dating for about three weeks.

Smiles

I had my fingers crossed for a "yes."

Ann

Eyes gleaming

I could barely wait for you to finish the question.

Smiles

But I had told myself to be composed with my answer.

Granville

Modest flamboyancy

When you accepted my invitation, I could literally see myself escorting you into the ball.

Ann

Excited

And as soon as I put the telephone down I jumped for joy. I could hear my roommate asking me what happened, but I was so happy until I couldn't respond.

Pause

I looked in my closet and scrambled through the clothes rack.

Pause

I found a dress I had purchased in California! I took it out and held it against my body as I looked into the mirror.

Pause

My roommate knew what the excitement was all about! "Gran, invited you to the Alpha's Ball?" she asked. By then I was jumping up and down with excitement. The only words coming out of my mouth were, "Yes, yes, yes!" Before we knew it, we were both holding hands, jumping with joy as if we were a cheering squad! It was a special occasion for me.

GRANVILLE listens attentively, ANN continues.

Let's see if I remember your fraternity attire of that night.

Places her right hand under her chin, pauses, remembering.

You were wearing a gold jacket.

Pause

White ruffled shirt and black slacks. That's it!

GRANVILLE

Breaks his silence

Don't forget that gold cummerbund!

Smile

Emphasizing that neat waistline.

Laughs

ANN

Laughs in a teasing manner

How could I forget that?

Quick touch on his hand in a teasing manner.

GRANVILLE

How well do I remember! Is that still one of your favorite past times?

ANN

I usually attend dinner dances sponsored by the alumni for fundraising events.

GRANVILLE

Serious expression appears on his face

We used to see some pretty good movies on campus.

Pause

There is one movie shown on campus I think I will always remember.

ANN

Bows her head and speaks softly

"Splendor in the Grass."

As she spoke the words, tenderness emerged in her voice.

Yes, Gran.

Pause

I remember.

GRANVILLE

I guess I will always remember that movie as a summary of what happened to our relationship.

ANN

Speaks in a maudlin tone

The movie was shown just a few weeks after our break-off.

GRANVILLE

Serious expression

In my mind, you were Natalie Wood.

ANN

And you were Warren Beatty.

GRANVILLE

Yes.

Pause

I loved you so much and I wanted you so completely.

ANN

But I just couldn't bring myself to break the principles my mother had instilled in me.

GRANVILLE

There was no doubt I knew I loved you more than anyone else, but the temptations were there.

ANN

Glances out the window

For a long time, Gran.

Pause

I could not understand how you could let temptation creep in to destroy the great love we had.

Silence

Granville

Head bowed for a second, he looks up

Even after Jean and I were married, I knew my feelings for you would not change.

Pause

After seeing, "Splendor in the Grass," I became even more concerned about you.

Ann

You mean you wanted to make sure I did not take a dive into the water. Like Natalie Wood?

Granville

Serious expression

I didn't know how badly you were taking the break-off.

Ann

It was bad.

Pause

To be honest, it was more than bad.

Granville

Clenched hands underneath his chin

I didn't know how to tell you…

Pause

about the mistake I had made.

Ann

Looks up for revelation

And that's why you gave those contrived reasons for the break-off?

Granville

Bows head

I was too hurt and too disappointed in myself to do otherwise.

Ann

I remember the day quite well.

Pause

As if it had just happened yesterday.

Pause

I was sitting in the rear of the classroom in my Tests and Measurements class.

Looks up at GRANVILLE.

Rose, a dorm mate during my freshman year, said she just had to tell me something. She said that her conscience would not let her keep it.

GRANVILLE

Concerned facial appearance

That's how you first heard about it?

ANN

Bows head in affirmative with hands slightly clenched, resting on the table

"Ann," she said. "You know Granville is getting married to a girl in Stamford Hall."

Looks up at GRANVILLE.

"He's marrying her," she said, "but he loves you."

GRANVILLE

Face of sorrow

That was true!

ANN

Unmoved

When Rose had finished telling me those words… I did not tarry. I got up and walked out of the classroom, immediately. I had forgotten about everything.

GRANVILLE

Looking intensely at ANN

Go on.

He urged.

ANN

Smiles

You know I didn't smoke. But the first stop I made was at the "Rec," where I purchased a pack of cigarettes.

Pause

And as I walked slowly to the dorm, I heard myself whispering a prayer: "Lord, please don't let this be true."

GRANVILLE

Rubs both hands across his face then rests them on the table

That was a shock.

Pause

And I guess it plagued my mind for many years.

ANN

And of course, I went through the various stages of lost love.

Pause

The can't eat, the can't sleep, and the other destructive behaviors.

Pause

But by spring I was able to begin dealing with what the winter storm had thrust upon me that February Day.

Pause

There were always the flashbacks to our love, but by April I had mustered enough strength to begin to look to brighter horizons.

GRANVILLE

Serious expression. Eye contact

To be honest with you, Ann…

Pause

My ship in April was still running on stormy waters, even though it was late spring.

Pause

I found myself in the same situation.

Silence

My love for you just dominated everything.

Glances out the window, then looks at ANN.

Jean and I were constantly having arguments and fights.

Silence

And you know why.

ANN

Look of understanding

Over me?

GRANVILLE

Bows head in affirmative

I couldn't control my feelings.

Pause

Sometimes I would tell her point blank that I loved you and I hadn't planned to marry her.

Ann

Direct eye contact

A few days after Rose gave me the sad news she spoke to me again about what had happened. "Regardless of what happens," she said, "Granville loves you."

Granville

Sincere smile

That was the truth.

Ann

Continues

Jean was always boasting in the dormitory, she said, about how she was going to get you if it was the last thing that she did.

Granville

A victim, yes.

Pause

But I have to be accountable for my own vulnerability to victimhood.

Ann

After you and Jean were married, Rose spoke to me again. She said, "Even though he is married to her, Gran will come back one day and tell you the truth about his love for you." She even said that she would bet me a silver dollar that the day would come soon.

Granville

Smiles

It did come soon.

Ann

Yes, I remember your telephone calls after the union.

Granville

Shakes his head

No, I mean the real issue.

Ann

You mean when you went to my mother's house to apologize to her about what had happened?

GRANVILLE

Yes.

Pause

But, I mean the crossroads when I had courageously come to grips with my life and my feelings.

ANN

Oh, you mean during the summer after you graduated.

GRANVILLE

Serious expression

Yes!

Pause

I had made up my mind.

Silence

I loved you, and I wanted to be married to you at any cost.

Pause

It was a tough decision, but I knew what I wanted.

Eye contact

But the question was, at that time, could I get what I so desperately wanted?

Pause

Remember?

ANN

I was avoiding you at all costs.

Pause

When I returned to the campus that June for summer school, my roommate, Virginia, had a message for me. "You've just returned today?" she asked. "Gran has been desperately looking for you." I was reluctant about seeing you, but she stressed the urgency of your request.

GRANVILLE

I was happy that you had agreed to see me.

Eye contact

It was my last hope of trying to bind our love.

ANN

Glances out the window

As I look back, I still had not gained complete control of life.

Granville

I felt like General Custer at his last stand.

Pause

I knew of no other way than to be just plain honest with you.

Ann

It had taken a lot out of me to stand up and face the whole campus alone.

Silence

Standing naively exposed, with everyone knowing the naked truth.

Pause

That, despite the fact that I was your sweetheart on campus, like an owl out of the night, you married another girl.

Pause

On campus, the day after the union, some students were congratulating me!

Silence

They were so sure that I was the person you had married.

Granville

Remorseful

Well, I had come to you on that summer night, hoping that the error could have been corrected.

Pause

I had to deal honestly with my conscience.

Ann

Slight smile appears

And you were so brave to take the stand.

Granville

I don't remember the exact words, but I do remember telling you I had received my commission as Second Lieutenant in the Air Force.

Silence

And I wanted to know if you would marry me. And I would get a divorce as soon as the baby was born. I had to know before I left so that I could put my official service papers in order.

Ann

Looks up and their eyes meet

I loved you, Gran. But I was torn between the impetus of my mother's philosophy and I had just overcome the hurt of that cold February day.

Granville

I remember your answer too well. You shared some of the pain you had endured. You said since I was married to Jean, I might as well stay married to her. Then you said when the time was right, you would meet that someone to marry.

Ann

Eye contact

After we kissed, your last words were…

Granville

Remember always that you were the one that I really loved.

Eye contact; tender smile

Ann

That's where we left off!

Granville

And here we are twenty years later on the same campus.

Ann

A slight smile appears on her face

On this campus, I experienced my greatest joy, and in 1964, it gave me my greatest pain. Now I can say that I've found the strength to return.

Shakes head in disbelief

My first time back in twenty years!

Granville

Envelops her hands and they both smile

I can't express my feelings about you. I'm just happy that we've had a chance to share our feelings after so many years.

Ann

Looks into his eyes and smiles with affection

Our feelings interlock. I think that it's safe to say that as we look back through the years, we've found strength to overcome the tears.

Granville

Glances out the window as he holds her hands gently

Do you have time to take a quick stroll across campus with me?

Ann

Pauses for a moment, then smiles

Why not! After all, we have grown as tall as the trees!

BLACKOUT

THE END

THE REUNION QUESTIONS

I. THOUGHT QUESTIONS

A. Granville stood in the window of Douglas Guest Hall, reminiscing about his old college days. Describe the mood.

B. Write a full description of Granville's character.

C. Was Granville basically an honest man? Why?

D. What kind of academic student was Granville in college?

E. What is the full name for the ROTC?

F. In what ways were George and Granville alike? How were they different?

G. Did George believe that the Vietnam War was a worthwhile cause?

H. Did the Vietnam War have an impact on male students in college?

I. Why were Granville's thoughts often dwelling in the past?

J. Was Granville happily married? Why? Or Why not?

K. What did Granville mean by the statement, "I guess there are some things all of us carry closely in our hearts, sometimes in life and I, being no exception, am guilty, too"?

L. What did George mean when he said to Granville, "Oh Pal, the torch is burning after twenty years"?

M. Was George able to help his friend, Granville, get a clearer perception of his problem? If so, how? Explain your answer.

II. PERIODS IN HISTORY

Choose a topic from below to outline and write a short essay.

A. John F. Kennedy was described as a charismatic leader. His intellect, charm, wit, and youth had won him the hearts of many Americans. Write a report describing the mood of the country during his term of Presidency.

B. The Vietnam War was an important issue in America. Prepare a report on the Pros and Cons of this war.

C. Male chauvinism became a very popular term in the United States. Research the origin of this term and prepare a written report.

D. Women's Liberation is still a current issue. Use the United States Congressional Records to compile a report on the progress of the ERA.

III. LIBRARY ASSIGNMENTS

A. Do a literary search on the English writer William Wordsworth. Locate his poem, "Ode: Intimations of Immortality From Recollections of Early Childhood." Refer to stanza X of the poem and write a composition explaining what you think the author meant by, "Splendor in the Grass." Show the relationship to Ann and Granville in "The Reunion."

B. Review the life and work of General George A. Custer. Write a composition describing what Granville meant in "The Reunion," when he said, "I felt like General Custer, making his last stand."

C. Review the movie "Splendor in the Grass," starring Natalie Woods and Warren Beatty. Write a synopsis of the movie and show the relationship of "The Reunion" to "Splendor in the Grass."

IV. DESCRIPTIVE ANALYSIS

A. Describe your favorite character in "The Reunion." Tell why you made this selection.

B. Describe the character you like least. Express your dislike for this character.

C. Describe your favorite scene in "The Reunion."

D. Describe the physical appearance and atmosphere of this college campus.

E. Describe the school spirit of the college students on this campus.

V. VOCABULARY

Write a synonym for the words below.

accountable

assassination

attire

chauvinism

digress

disguise

ecstasy

flamboyancy

gesticulate

luminous

impetus

instill

maudlin

naïve

perception

regression

remorseful

retort

philosophy of life

vulnerable

VI. WRITE YOUR INTERPRETATION

The closing line of "The Reunion" was "After all, we have grown as tall as the trees!"

VII. MULTIPLE CHOICE

Complete each statement below by selecting the correct letter. Write your choice in the blank provided.

____ 1. Where did George and his family live?
(a) Texas (b) Washington, D.C. (c) Cincinnati, OH
(d) Baltimore, MD

____ 2. Granville was a Major in the:
(a) Army b) Air Force (c) Marines (d) Navy

____ 3. George and Granville had been soldiers in:
(a) W.W. II (b) Korean War (c) Nicaragua Conflict
(d) Vietnam War

____ 4. ROTC is an abbreviation for:
(a) Reserved Offices Training Core (b) Reservation Officers Training Camp (c) Reserved Officers Training Corps
(d) Reserved Official Teaching Core

____ 5. A student in engineering should have a strong background in:
(a) mathematics and science (b) English and social studies
(c) writing and journalism (d) geography and literature

____ 6. Granville's war record earned him a:
(a) silver star (b) meritorious award (c) bronze medal
(d) purple heart

____ 7. The president who was assassinated when Granville was in college was:
(a) Garfield (b) McKinley (c) Kennedy (d) Lincoln

____ 8. What General in U. S. History is known for "making his last stand"?
(a) Sherman (b) Custer (c) Granville (d) Patton

____ 9. The female actress who starred in the movie, "Splendor in the Grass" was:
(a) Raquel Welch (b) Brook Shields (c) Natalie Woods
(d) Diann Carroll

____ 10. Granville had returned to the college campus for:
(a) an engineering conference (b) Recruitment
(c) ROTC conference (d) college homecoming

____ 11. George's wife's name in "The Reunion" was:
(a) Barbara (b) Jean (c) Ann (d) Rose

____ 12. The person who first told Ann about Granville's plans for marriage was:
(a) Jean (b) Virginia (c) Barbara (d) Rose

____ 13. What academic class was Ann in when she was first told the wedding plans?
(a) American Literature (b) Tests & Measurements
(c) American History (d) Trigonometry

____ 14. In 1984, Granville was stationed in Andrews Air Force Base located in:
(a) Washington, D.C. (b) Maryland (c) Texas (d) Ohio

____ 15. After the war, George pursued a career in:
(a) managing his own business (b) engineering
(c) ROTC instruction (d) computer analysis

____ 16. In "The Reunion," Granville had:
(a) four boys (b) two girls & two boys (c) four girls
(d) three girls, one boy

____ 17. The name of Granville's college football team was:
(a) Hummingbirds (b) Golden Tigers (c) Jets (d) Falcons

____ 18. The coach for Granville's college football team was:
(a) Bowie (b) Bowers (c) Bowar (d) Bonwire

____ 19. The term "alumni" is used to identify a people who are:
(a) freshmen (b) sophomores (c) graduates (d) juniors

____ 20. George told his wife and children that he would meet them at the:
(a) hotel (b) library (c) museum (d) football stadium

____ 21. In what year did a U.S. Presidential assassination occur?
(a) 1973 (b) 1960 (c) 1963 (d) 1970

____ 22. Granville probably married Jean because:
(a) he was in love (b) he felt obligated to do so
(c) she was his college sweetheart (d) his parents approved

____ 23. How many children did George have?
(a) three (b) two (c) one (d) unknown

____ 24. How many U. S. Presidents were assassinated in the decade of the 1960s?
(a) one (b) two (c) three (d) none

____ 25. Who did Granville escort to chapel for memorial services?
(a) Jean (b) Virginia (d) Ann (d) Rose

VIII: ORGANIZATION: What Happened First?

Directions: Place the statements below in sequential order. Use numbers 1-9 to indicate your answers. The first event would be assigned #1 and the last event would be assigned #9. Place your numbers in the blanks provided.

____ 1. The waiter rolled a tray into Granville's room.

____ 2. Granville's classmate, George, came to visit him.

____ 3. Gran and Ann left the lounge.

____ 4. Ann and Gran had a long conversation in the lounge.

____ 5. Granville stood in the window reminiscing the assassination and college days.

____ 6. Granville got dressed to begin his day's schedule.

____ 7. Ann and Gran took a stroll across the college campus.

____ 8. Ann and Gran embraced in the lobby.

____ 9. Granville saw a lady talking on the telephone.

IX. FACT OR OPINION

Directions: Place the statements below in sequential order. Use numbers 1-9 to indicate your answers. The first event would be assigned #1 and the last event would be assigned #9. Place your numbers in the blank provided.

____ 1. The Vietnam War was not worthwhile.

____ 2. Many lives were lost in the Vietnam War.

____ 3. President John F. Kennedy was assassinated.

____ 4. The security system did not do a good job in protecting President Kennedy.

____ 5. Natalie Woods was the best female actress in Hollywood in the 1960s.

____ 6. Natalie Woods was the leading female star in "Splendor in the Grass."

____ 7. George A. Custer was the best General in American history.

____ 8. George A. Custer was a General in the U.S. Army.

Addendum

Don't Quit

Anonymous

When things go wrong,
As they sometimes will,
When the road you're trudging
Seems uphill,
When the funds are low,
And the debts are high,
And you want to smile,
But you have to sigh,
When care is pressing you down a bit,
Rest if you must,
But don't you quit.

Life is queer with its twists and turns,
As everyone of us sometimes learns,
And many a failure turns about,
When he might have won had he stuck it out;
Don't give up though the pace seems slow,
You may succeed with another blow.

Success is failure turned inside out,
The silver tint of the clouds of doubt,
And you never can tell how close you are,
It may be near when it seems so far;
So stick to the fight when you're hardest hit,
It's when things seem worse,
Then you must not QUIT.

Lord Why Did You Make Me Black?

by RuNell Ni Ebo

Lord, Lord
Why did You make me Black?
Why did You make someone
The world wants to hold back?

Black is the color of dirty clothes,
The color of grimy hands and feet
Black is the color of darkness,
The color of tire-beaten streets.

Why did You give me thick lips,
A broad nose and kinky hair?
Why did You make someone
Who receives the hatred stare?

Black is the color of the bruised eye
When someone gets hurt.
Black is the color of darkness,
Black is the color of dirt.

How come my bone structure's so thick,
My hips and cheeks are high?
How come my eyes are brown
And not the color of daylight sky?

Why do people think I'm useless?
How come I feel so used?
Why do some people see my skin
And think I should be abused?

Lord, I just don't understand.
What is it about my skin?
Why do some people want to hate me
And not know the person within?

Black is what people are "listed"
When others want to keep them away.
Black is the color of shadows cast.
Black is the end of the day.

Lord, you know my own people mistreat me
And I know this just ain't right.
They don't like my hair.
They say I'm too dark or too light.

Lord, don't You think it's time for You
To make a change?
Why don't You re-do creation and
Make every one the same?

God Answered

Why did I make you black?
Why did I make you black?
Get off your knees and look around.
Tell me, what do you see?
I didn't make you in the image of darkness
I made you in the likeness of ME!

I made you the color of coal from which
Beautiful diamonds are formed.
I made you the color of oil, the black
gold that keeps people warm.

I made you from the rich, dark earth that
Can grow the food you need.
Your color's the same as the black
Stallion, a majestic animal is he.
I didn't make you in the image of darkness.
I made you in the likeness of ME!

All the colors of the heavenly rainbow
Can be found throughout every nation.
But when all of those colors were
blended, you became my greatest creation.

Your hair is the texture of lamb's wool.
Such a humble little creature is he.
I am the Shepherd who watches them.
I am the One who will watch over thee.

You are the color of midnight sky.
There is a smile hidden behind your pain.
That's why your cheeks are so high.

You are the color of dark clouds formed,
When I send My strongest weather.
I made your lips full so when you kiss the
One that you love, they will remember.

Your stature is strong, your bone
Structure thick to withstand the burdens
Of time.
The reflection you see in the mirror…
The image that looks back is MINE.

Note: Remember—"What you see with your eyes is colored by the condition of your heart." A. R. Bernard, Sr.

RESOURCES FOR YOUNG PEOPLE

Addams, Jane. *The Spirit of Youth & the City Streets*, LC72-78862, 192 p. 12.50 (ISBN 0-252-00276-8). U of Ill Pr.

Anderson, D.S. & Blakers, C. eds. *Youth: Transition & Social Research*. LC82-73642.(Illus.), 204 p. 1984, pap. Text ed. 10.95x (ISBN-7081-1028-2) ANU Pr. Barnes, Grace M. compiled by *Alcohol & Youth: A Comprehensive Bibliography*, LC82-15397, xvi, 432 p. 1982, lib. Bdg. 45.00(ISBN 0-313-23136-2, BAY) Greenwood.

Bell, Howard M. *Youth Tell Their Story: A Study of the Conditions & Attitudes of Young People in Maryland Between the Ages of 16 and 24*. facsimile ed. LC74-1665.(Children & Youth Ser.: Social Problems & Social Policy)290 p. 1974. Reprint of 1938 ed. 24.50(ISBN 0-405-05946-9). Ayer Co.

Bossard, James H. & Boll, Eleanor S., eds. *Adolescents in Wartime*. Facsimile ed. LC 74-1668.(Children & Youth Serv.). 180 p. 1974. Repr. Of 1944 ed. 18.00x (ISBN 0-405-05947), Ayer Co.

Brody, Eugene B. *Minority Group Adolescents in the United States*. LC 78-20769. 256 p. 1979. Repr. Of 1968 ed. Lib. Bdg. 14.50(ISBN 0-88275-849-7) Krieger.

Brown, Sheldon S. *A Guide to Study Children & Adolescents*. 2nd ed. 1978, pap. Text Ed. 9.995(ISBN 0-8403-1304-7). Kendall Hunt.

Campbell. *How to Really Love Your Teenager*. 1982. 4.50 (ISBN 0-88207-274-9) Victor Books.

Coleman, James S. et al. *The Adolescent Society: The Social Life of the Teenager & Its Impact on Education*. LC81- 1737. Illus. xvi, 368 p. 1981. Repr. Of 1961 ed. Lib. Bdg. 35.000x (ISBN 0-313-22934-1, COADS). Greenwood.

Gonger, John. *Adolescence: Generation Under Pressure* (Life Cycle Set). 1980, pap. Text ed. 4.761(ISBN 0-06- 384744-2, Harp C) Har-Row.

Gordon, Sol. *The Teenage Survival Book: The Complete Revised, Updated Edition of YOU* 150 p. 1981. pap 9.95 (ISBN 0-8129-0972-0). Times Bks.

Foster, Sallie. *The One Girl in Ten: A Self Portrait of the Teenage Mother*, LC 8169000. 159 p.(Orig.) gr. 7-12). 1981. pap. 5.00(ISBN 0-9607108-1-7) Arbor Claremont.

Lindsay, Jeanne W. *Teens Parenting: The Challenge of Babies and Toddlers.* LC 80-84900.(Illus.); pap. 9.95(ISBN 0-960934-06-7); tchr's guide 5.95(ISBN 0-930934-09-1); wkbk. 2.50(ISBN 0-930934-08-3). Morning Glory.

Lux, J. Scott. *How to Help Your Teenager Become Themselves*. LC 82-170628. 140 p. 1982. pap. 7.95 (ISBN 0-9609324-0-2). Family Friends.

Mihaly, Mary E. *Getting Your Own: A Guide to Growing Up Assertively.* LC 78-27050. 180 p.(gr. 7 p.). 1979. 6.95(ISBN 0-87131-285-9). M. Evans.

Steiner, Rudolf. Waldorf *Education for Adolescence*. 1980. pap. 9.75x (ISBN-96492-37-8, Pub. By Kolisko Archives). St. George Bk Serv. 1983. 15.00(ISBN 0- 8134, 2134-9). Interstate.